First World War
and Army of Occupation
War Diary
France, Belgium and Germany

66 DIVISION
199 Infantry Brigade
Manchester Regiment
2/7th Battalion
6 March 1917 - 31 July 1918

WO95/3145/2

The Naval & Military Press Ltd
www.nmarchive.com
Published in association with The National Archives

Published by

The Naval & Military Press Ltd

Unit 10 Ridgewood Industrial Park,

Uckfield, East Sussex,

TN22 5QE England

Tel: +44 (0) 1825 749494

www.naval-military-press.com

www.nmarchive.com

This diary has been reprinted in facsimile from the original. Any imperfections are inevitably reproduced and the quality may fall short of modern type and cartographic standards.

Contents

Document type	Place/Title	Date From	Date To
Heading	WO95/3145/2 2/7 Battalion Manchester Regiment		
Heading	66th Division 199th Infy Bde 2-7th Bn Manch Regt Mar 1917-Jly 1918 1917 Sep-1916 Feb 1917 Mar-1918 Jly		
War Diary	Colchester	06/03/1917	06/03/1917
War Diary	Boulogne	07/03/1917	07/03/1917
War Diary	Berguette	13/03/1917	14/03/1917
War Diary	Paradis	14/03/1917	16/03/1917
War Diary	Beuvrey	17/03/1917	18/03/1917
War Diary	Cambrin	19/03/1917	23/03/1917
War Diary	Annequin	26/03/1917	27/03/1917
War Diary	Hohenzollern	28/03/1917	29/03/1917
War Diary	Cambrin Right	30/03/1917	31/03/1917
Map	Hohenzollern Sector Cambrin Right		
Operation(al) Order(s)	2/7th Battalion Manchester Regiment Order No. 1.	13/03/1917	13/03/1917
Operation(al) Order(s)	2/7th Battalion Manchester Regiment Order No. 2	15/03/1917	15/03/1917
Operation(al) Order(s)	2/7th Battalion Manchester Regiment Order No. 3.	18/03/1917	18/03/1917
Operation(al) Order(s)	2/7th Battalion Manchester Regiment Order No. 4.	22/03/1917	22/03/1917
Operation(al) Order(s)	2/7th Battalion Manchester Regiment Order No. 5.	26/03/1917	26/03/1917
Miscellaneous	Relief Of Hohenzollern Sub-Sector		
Operation(al) Order(s)	2/7th Battalion Manchester Regiment Order No. 6.	30/03/1917	30/03/1917
Miscellaneous	Time Table And Routes On April		
Miscellaneous	2/7th Bn Manchester Regt. Daily Intelligence Report from 7.0 am 28.3.17 to 7.0 am 29.3.17	29/03/1917	29/03/1917
Miscellaneous	2/7th Bn. Manchester Regt Daily Intelligence Report from 7.0 am 29.3.17 to 7.0 am 30.3.17	29/03/1917	29/03/1917
Miscellaneous	2/7th Bn. Manchester Regt Daily Intelligence Report from 7.0 am 30.3.17 to 7.0 am 31.3.17	31/03/1917	31/03/1917
Miscellaneous	2/7th Bn. Manchester Regt Daily Intelligence Report from 7.0 am 31.3.17 to 3.0 pm 31.3.17	31/03/1917	31/03/1917
Miscellaneous	2/7th Bn. Manchester Regt Supplement to Daily Intelligence Report from 7.0 am 31.3.17 to 3.0 pm 31.3.17	31/03/1917	31/03/1917
Heading	War Diary of 2/7 Bn The Manchester Regt. From March 6th To March 31st 1917 Volume 1.		
Miscellaneous	T.P.R's		
Miscellaneous	Time Table And Routes On March 31st Relief Of Cambrin Right		
Miscellaneous	2/7th Bn. Manchester Regiment		
Miscellaneous	Operation Orders		
Diagram etc	Appendix B		
Miscellaneous	Casualty Returns		
Miscellaneous	2/7th Battalion Manchester Regiment.	01/04/1917	01/04/1917
Miscellaneous	Maps		
Heading	War Diary of 2/7th Bn. The Manchester Regt. From April 1st 1917 To April 30th 1917 Volume 2		
War Diary	Annequin	01/04/1917	03/04/1917
War Diary	Cambrin Right	04/04/1917	08/04/1917
War Diary	Noyelles	08/04/1917	11/04/1917
War Diary	Cambrin Right	12/04/1917	15/04/1917

War Diary	Village Line	16/04/1917	19/04/1917
War Diary	Cambrin Right	21/04/1917	27/04/1917
War Diary	Village Line	29/04/1917	30/04/1917
Operation(al) Order(s)	2/7th Battalion Manchester Regiment Order No. 7.	03/04/1917	03/04/1917
Operation(al) Order(s)	2/7th Battalion Manchester Regiment Order No. 8.	07/04/1917	07/04/1917
Miscellaneous	Relief of Cambrin Right 2/7th Manc R. by 2/8th Manc R. on 8/4/17		
Miscellaneous	Time Table Routes On April 12th Relief Day		
Operation(al) Order(s)	2/7th Battalion Manchester Regiment Order No. 9.	11/04/1917	11/04/1917
Operation(al) Order(s)	2/7th Battalion Manchester Regiment Order No. 10.	15/04/1917	15/04/1917
Miscellaneous	After Order.	15/04/1917	15/04/1917
Miscellaneous	Relief Day	16/04/1917	16/04/1917
Operation(al) Order(s)	2/7th Battalion Manchester Regiment Order No. 11.	10/04/1917	10/04/1917
Operation(al) Order(s)	2/7th Battalion Manchester Regiment Order No. 12.	23/04/1917	23/04/1917
Operation(al) Order(s)	2/7th Battalion Manchester Regiment Order No. 13.	27/04/1917	27/04/1917
Heading	Confidential Vol 3 War Diary of 2/7th Bn The Manchester Regt From Mar 1st 1917 To May 31st 1917		
Miscellaneous	28-4-17 Relief Day	28/04/1917	28/04/1917
War Diary	Fosse House	01/05/1917	01/05/1917
War Diary	Cambrin Left	02/05/1917	06/05/1917
War Diary	Noyelles	08/05/1917	09/05/1917
War Diary	Cambrin Right	14/05/1917	17/05/1917
War Diary	Annequin	23/05/1917	26/05/1917
War Diary	Cambrin Right	27/05/1917	31/05/1917
Operation(al) Order(s)	2/7th Battalion Manchester Regiment Order No. 19.	04/05/1917	04/05/1917
Operation(al) Order(s)	2/7th Battalion Manchester Regiment Order No. 16.	11/08/1917	11/08/1917
Miscellaneous	Route Table	11/05/1917	11/05/1917
Operation(al) Order(s)	2/7th Battalion Manchester Regiment Order No. 16	11/05/1917	11/05/1917
Miscellaneous	Route Table	11/05/1917	11/05/1917
Operation(al) Order(s)	2/7th Battalion Manchester Regiment Order No. 18.	11/05/1917	11/05/1917
Miscellaneous	Route Table	11/05/1917	11/05/1917
War Diary	Cambrin Right	01/06/1917	05/06/1917
War Diary	Noyelles	05/06/1917	10/06/1917
War Diary	Cambrin Rt.	12/06/1917	16/06/1917
War Diary	Annequin	21/06/1917	21/06/1917
War Diary	Lapugnoy	24/06/1917	24/06/1917
War Diary	Petit Synthe	26/06/1917	30/06/1917
Miscellaneous	Relief Day 5.6.17.	05/06/1917	05/06/1917
Operation(al) Order(s)	2/7th Battalion Manchester Regiment Order No. 20.	10/06/1917	10/06/1917
Miscellaneous	Relief Day.	11/06/1917	11/06/1917
Miscellaneous	Relief Table.	17/06/1917	17/06/1917
Operation(al) Order(s)	2/7th Battalion Manchester Regiment Order No. 21.	16/06/1917	16/06/1917
Operation(al) Order(s)	2/7th Battalion Manchester Regiment Operation Order No. 22.	21/06/1917	21/06/1917
Operation(al) Order(s)	2/7th Battalion Manchester Regiment Operation Order No. 23	24/06/1917	24/06/1917
Miscellaneous	Secret No.2		
Miscellaneous	2/7th Battalion Manchester Regiment.		
War Diary	Petite Synthe	01/07/1917	08/07/1917
War Diary	Teteghem	09/07/1917	11/07/1917
War Diary	Ghyvelde	12/07/1917	14/07/1917
War Diary	Coxyde Bains	15/07/1917	20/07/1917
War Diary	Camp Lefevre	21/07/1917	25/07/1917
War Diary	Nieuport	26/07/1917	30/07/1917
War Diary	Left Sub Sector Lombartzyde	31/07/1917	31/07/1917

Operation(al) Order(s)	2/7th Battalion Manchester Regiment Operation Order No. 24.	06/07/1917	06/07/1917
Operation(al) Order(s)	2/7th Battalion Manchester Regiment Operation Order No. 25.	11/07/1917	11/07/1917
Miscellaneous	2/7th Battalion Manchester Regiment Operation Order No. 26.	14/07/1917	14/07/1917
Miscellaneous	2/7th Battalion Manchester Regiment Order No. 27.	20/07/1917	20/07/1917
Operation(al) Order(s)	2/7th Battalion Manchester Regiment Order No. 28.	24/07/1917	24/07/1917
Heading	War Diary of 2/7 Bn The Manchester Regt From 1.8.17 To 31.8.17 Volume VI		
Heading	War Diary of 2/7th Battn The Manchester Regt. From August 1st 1917 To August 31st 1917 Volume No-5		
War Diary	Lombartzyde (left) Sub Sector	01/08/1917	03/08/1917
War Diary	St. Idesbald	04/08/1917	09/08/1917
War Diary	Oost Dunkerke Bains	10/08/1917	11/08/1917
War Diary	Nieuport Bains (Right) Sub Sector	12/08/1917	20/08/1917
War Diary	Coxyde Bains	22/08/1917	26/08/1917
War Diary	La Panne	27/08/1917	31/08/1917
Operation(al) Order(s)	2/7th Battalion Manchester Regiment Order No. 30.	03/08/1917	03/08/1917
Operation(al) Order(s)	2/7th Battalion Manchester Regiment Order No. 31.	09/08/1917	09/08/1917
Operation(al) Order(s)	2/7th Battalion Manchester Regiment Order No. 32.	11/08/1917	11/08/1917
Miscellaneous	2/7th Battalion Manchester Regiment.	11/08/1917	11/08/1917
Operation(al) Order(s)	2/7th Battalion Manchester Regiment Order No. 33.	22/08/1917	22/08/1917
Miscellaneous	2/7th Battalion Manchester Regiment Order No. 34		
Operation(al) Order(s)	2/7th Battalion Manchester Regiment Order No 35.	20/08/1917	20/08/1917
Heading	War Diary of 2/7 Bn Manch Regt From 1.9.17 To 30.9.17 Volume VII		
War Diary	La Panne	02/09/1917	02/09/1917
War Diary	St Idesbald	03/09/1917	19/09/1917
War Diary	Oost Dunkerke	18/09/1917	24/09/1917
War Diary	St Idesbald	25/09/1917	25/09/1917
War Diary	Ghyvelde	26/09/1917	26/09/1917
War Diary	Bandringhem	28/09/1917	28/09/1917
Miscellaneous	Operation Orders.		
Operation(al) Order(s)	2/7th Battalion Manchester Regiment. Order No. 37.	02/09/1917	02/09/1917
Operation(al) Order(s)	2/7th Battalion Manchester Regiment Order No. 38.	18/09/1917	18/09/1917
Operation(al) Order(s)	2/7th Battalion Manchester Regiment Order No. 39.	24/09/1917	24/09/1917
Operation(al) Order(s)	2/7th Battalion Manchester Regiment Order No. 40	25/09/1917	25/09/1917
Operation(al) Order(s)	2/7th Battalion Manchester Regiment Order No. 41.	28/09/1917	28/09/1917
Operation(al) Order(s)	2/7th Battalion Manchester Regiment Order No. 43		
Heading	War Diary Of 2/7th Bn. Manch Regt. Volume-VIII October 1917		
War Diary	Brandringhem	01/10/1917	05/10/1917
War Diary	E Of Ypres	06/10/1917	10/10/1917
War Diary	Meningate	10/10/1917	10/10/1917
War Diary	Brandhoek	11/10/1917	11/10/1917
War Diary	Arques	13/10/1917	31/10/1917
Miscellaneous	2/7th Battalion Manchester Regiment Inspection Order.		
Operation(al) Order(s)	2/7th Battalion Manchester Regiment Order No. 42.	02/10/1917	02/10/1917
Heading	War Diary of 2/7th Battn The Manchester Regt. From Nov 1st 1917 To Nov 30th 1917 Volume 8		
War Diary	Arques	01/11/1917	01/11/1917
War Diary	Staple	07/11/1917	07/11/1917
War Diary	Ebblinghem	09/11/1917	09/11/1917
War Diary	Westoutre	09/11/1917	09/11/1917
War Diary	Ypres	10/11/1917	24/11/1917

War Diary	Berthen	26/11/1917	30/11/1917
Operation(al) Order(s)	2/7th Battalion Manchester Regiment Order No. 43	01/11/1917	01/11/1917
Operation(al) Order(s)	2/7th Battalion Manchester Regiment Order No. 44	07/11/1917	07/11/1917
Operation(al) Order(s)	2/7th Battalion Manchester Regiment Order No. 45	08/11/1917	08/11/1917
Operation(al) Order(s)	2/7th Battalion Manchester Regiment Order No. 46.	10/11/1917	10/11/1917
War Diary	2/7th Battalion Manchester Regiment Order No. 47.	23/11/1917	23/11/1917
Operation(al) Order(s)	2/7th Battalion Manchester Regiment Order No. 48.	28/11/1917	28/11/1917
Heading	War Diary of 2/7th Battn The Manchester Regt From-Decber 1st 1917 To Decber 31st 1917 Volume 9		
War Diary	Caestre Area	01/12/1917	15/12/1917
War Diary	Ypres Area	15/12/1917	30/12/1917
Miscellaneous	Relief Table		
Operation(al) Order(s)	2/7th Battalion Manchester Regiment Order No. 49.	15/12/1917	15/12/1917
Operation(al) Order(s)	2/7th Battalion Manchester Regiment Order No. 50.	30/12/1917	30/12/1917
Heading	War Diary of 2/7th Manchester Regiment. From 1st Jan To 31st Jan 1918 Vol-XI		
War Diary	Ypres Area	01/01/1918	01/01/1918
War Diary	Caestre Area	02/01/1918	11/01/1918
War Diary	Potijze Area.	12/01/1918	18/01/1918
War Diary	Line	20/01/1918	22/01/1918
War Diary	Vancouver Camp	23/01/1918	28/01/1918
War Diary	Line	29/01/1918	31/01/1918
Miscellaneous	2/7th Battalion Manchester Regiment. Warning Order.		
Operation(al) Order(s)	2/7th Battalion Manchester Regiment Order No. 52.	09/01/1918	09/01/1918
Operation(al) Order(s)	2/7th Battalion Manchester Regiment Order No. 54.	17/01/1918	17/01/1918
Operation(al) Order(s)	2/7th Battalion Manchester Regiment Order No. 55.	21/01/1918	21/01/1918
Miscellaneous	Relief Of 2/7th Bn. Manchester Regt.		
Operation(al) Order(s)	2/7th Battalion Manchester Regiment Order No. 56.	27/01/1918	27/01/1918
Miscellaneous	Relief Table		
Miscellaneous	Working Party Table.		
Heading	2/7th Bn Manch R. War Diary 1st Feb To 28th Feb Volume XII		
War Diary	Anzac Line	01/02/1918	09/02/1918
War Diary	Potijze Vancouner Area	10/02/1918	11/02/1918
War Diary	Proven Area	11/02/1918	18/02/1918
War Diary	Harbonniers Area	19/02/1918	24/02/1918
War Diary	Villiers Carbonnel Hancourt	25/02/1918	27/02/1918
War Diary	Vendelles	28/02/1918	28/02/1918
Miscellaneous	Reference Battalion Operation Order No. 50	10/02/1918	10/02/1918
Heading	2/7th Battalion Manchester Regiment March 1918		
Heading	War Diary of 2/7th Bn Manchester Regt From March 1st 1918 To March 31st 1918		
War Diary	Vendelles	01/03/1918	02/03/1918
War Diary	Line	02/03/1918	22/03/1918
War Diary	Montigny	20/03/1918	20/03/1918
War Diary	Jeancourt	22/03/1918	22/03/1918
War Diary	Barleux	23/03/1918	23/03/1918
War Diary	Biaches	24/03/1918	25/03/1918
War Diary	Herbecourt	26/03/1918	28/03/1918
War Diary	Ignancourt	29/03/1918	30/03/1918
Operation(al) Order(s)	2/7th Bn. Manch. R. Order No. 64	01/03/1918	01/03/1918
Operation(al) Order(s)	2/7th Battalion Manchester Regiment Operation Order No 65.	05/03/1918	05/03/1918
Operation(al) Order(s)	2/7th Bn. Manchester Regt. Operation Order No. 66.	13/03/1918	13/03/1918
Miscellaneous	Appendix A		
Miscellaneous	2/7th Battalion Manchester Regiment		

Operation(al) Order(s)	2/7 Bn. Manchester Regt Operation Order No. 57		
Operation(al) Order(s)	2/7 Bn. Manchester Regt Operation Order No. 58		
Operation(al) Order(s)	2/7 Bn. Manchester Regt Operation Order No. 59		
Operation(al) Order(s)	2/7th Battalion Manchester Regiment Operation Order No. 60.		
Operation(al) Order(s)	2/7th Bn. Manch. R. Order No. 61		
Operation(al) Order(s)	2/7th Bn Manch. R. Order No. 62.		
Operation(al) Order(s)	2/7th Battalion Manchester Regiment Order No. 63.	26/02/1918	26/02/1918
Miscellaneous	List Of Officers		
Heading	War Diary of 2/7th Bn. Manchester Regt. From April 1st 1918 To April 30th 1918 (Volume II)		
War Diary	Pissy	01/04/1918	02/04/1918
War Diary	Ailly	04/04/1918	04/04/1918
War Diary	Coulenvillers	06/04/1918	28/04/1918
Miscellaneous	Manchester Composite Battalion Move Order No. 1.	22/04/1918	22/04/1918
Operation(al) Order(s)	2/7th Battalion Manchester Regiment. Order No. 1.	26/04/1918	26/04/1918
Operation(al) Order(s)	2/7th Battalion Manchester Regiment Move Order No. 3.		
Miscellaneous	2/7th Battalion Manchester Regiment.	27/04/1918	27/04/1918
Heading	War Diary of 2/7th Manchester Regt. From May 1st 1918 To May 31st 1918 (Volume III)		
War Diary	Escuilles	02/05/1918	03/05/1918
War Diary	Watiehurt	09/05/1918	09/05/1918
War Diary	Lancheres	11/05/1918	11/05/1918
War Diary	Brutelles	12/05/1918	22/05/1918
War Diary	Montieres	24/05/1918	25/05/1918
Operation(al) Order(s)	2/7th Battalion Manchester Regiment. Order No. 4.	01/05/1918	01/05/1918
Operation(al) Order(s)	2/7th Battalion Manchester Regiment. Move Order No. 5.	31/05/1918	31/05/1918
War Diary	Boubert	01/06/1918	01/06/1918
War Diary	Woignarue	07/06/1918	07/06/1918
War Diary	Acheux	17/06/1918	17/06/1918
War Diary	Montieres	21/06/1918	21/06/1918
War Diary	Campagne	22/06/1918	22/06/1918
War Diary	Ouville	23/06/1918	23/06/1918
War Diary	Epagne	26/06/1918	26/06/1918
War Diary	Ailly	27/06/1918	27/06/1918
Operation(al) Order(s)	2/7th Battalion Manchester Regiment. Move Order No. 51.	06/06/1918	06/06/1918
Operation(al) Order(s)	2/7th Battalion Manchester Regiment. Move Order No. 53.	16/06/1918	16/06/1918
Operation(al) Order(s)	Move Order No. 1.	26/06/1918	26/06/1918
Heading	War Diary of 2/7th Bn Manchester Regt From 1st July 1918 To July 31st 1918 Vol XVI		
War Diary	Gorenflos	01/07/1918	01/07/1918
War Diary	Erancieres	20/07/1918	20/07/1918
War Diary	Haudricourt	22/07/1918	31/07/1918

WO/95/3145/2

2/7 Battalion Manchester Regiment

66TH DIVISION

199TH INFY BDE

2-7TH BN MANCH REGT

~~MAR 1917 - JLY 1918~~

1915 SEP — 1916 FEB

1917 MAR — 1918 JLY

DISBANDED

Instructions regarding War Diaries and Intelligence Summaries are contained in F. S. Regs., Part II. and the Staff Manual respectively. Title Pages will be prepared in manuscript.

WAR DIARY
or and
INTELLIGENCE SUMMARY
(Erase heading not required.)

Army Form C. 2118.

ORDERLY ROOM. 1 APR 1917 2/7th BATTALION MANCHESTER REGT.

Place	Date	Hour	Summary of Events and Information	Remarks and references to Appendices
COLCHESTER	6/3/17	2 AM	Bn leave COLCHESTER NORTH STATION	
" "	"	11 AM	arrived FOLKESTONE	
			Sailed on S.S. Arundel for BOULOGNE on arrival proceeded OSTROHOVE CAMP	
BOULOGNE	7/3/17	2-30 AM	Bn left BOULOGNE for BERGUETTE	
" "	"	5 PM	arrived BERGUETTE into billets	
BERGUETTE	13/3/17	4-30 PM	Order No 1 issued for move to billets at PARADIS	
" "	14/3/17	9-30 AM	Moved to PARADIS	
PARADIS	" "	2 PM	arrived PARADIS	
" "	15/3/17	10 PM	Order No 2 issued for move to BEUVRY.	
" "	16/3/17	1-30 PM	arrived BEUVREY	
BEUVREY	17/3/17	—	Received orders to take up left sector of CAMBRIN SECTOR	
	18/3/17	10 AM	Order No 3 issued	
CAMBRIN	19/3/17	10 AM	Relieved 1st NORFOLK REGT in CAMBRIN LEFT SECTOR	
" "	20/3/17	AM	Casualties 2 men wounded	
" "	21/3/17	1 PM	" " 3 men killed (buried by TM falling on TUNNEL) 2 wounded 1 accidentally wounded	
" "	22/3/17	11 AM	" " 1 man wounded	
" "	23/3/17	4 AM	OPERATION ORDER No 4 issued	
" "	" "	2 PM	Bn relieved by 2/8 Bn M/c Regt. Bn in Reserve at ANNIQUIN	
ANNEQUIN	26/3/17	11 PM	Order No 5 issued	
" "	27/3/17	10 AM	Relieved 9th Leicester Regiment in HOHENZOLLERN-SUBSECTOR	
HOHENZOLLERN	28/3/17	4 PM	Casualties 4 OR wounded 1 OR wounded (self inflicted) 1 OR killed	
" "	29/3/17	9 AM	" " 1 OR killed	
CAMBRIN RIGHT	30/3/17	—	" " 1 OR died of wounds 6 OR wounded Order No 6 issued Sub Sector re-named CAMBRIN RIGHT	
	31/3/17	10 AM	" " 1 OR wounded. Bn in SUPPORT	

[signature] Comdg 2/7th Bn Manch. R.

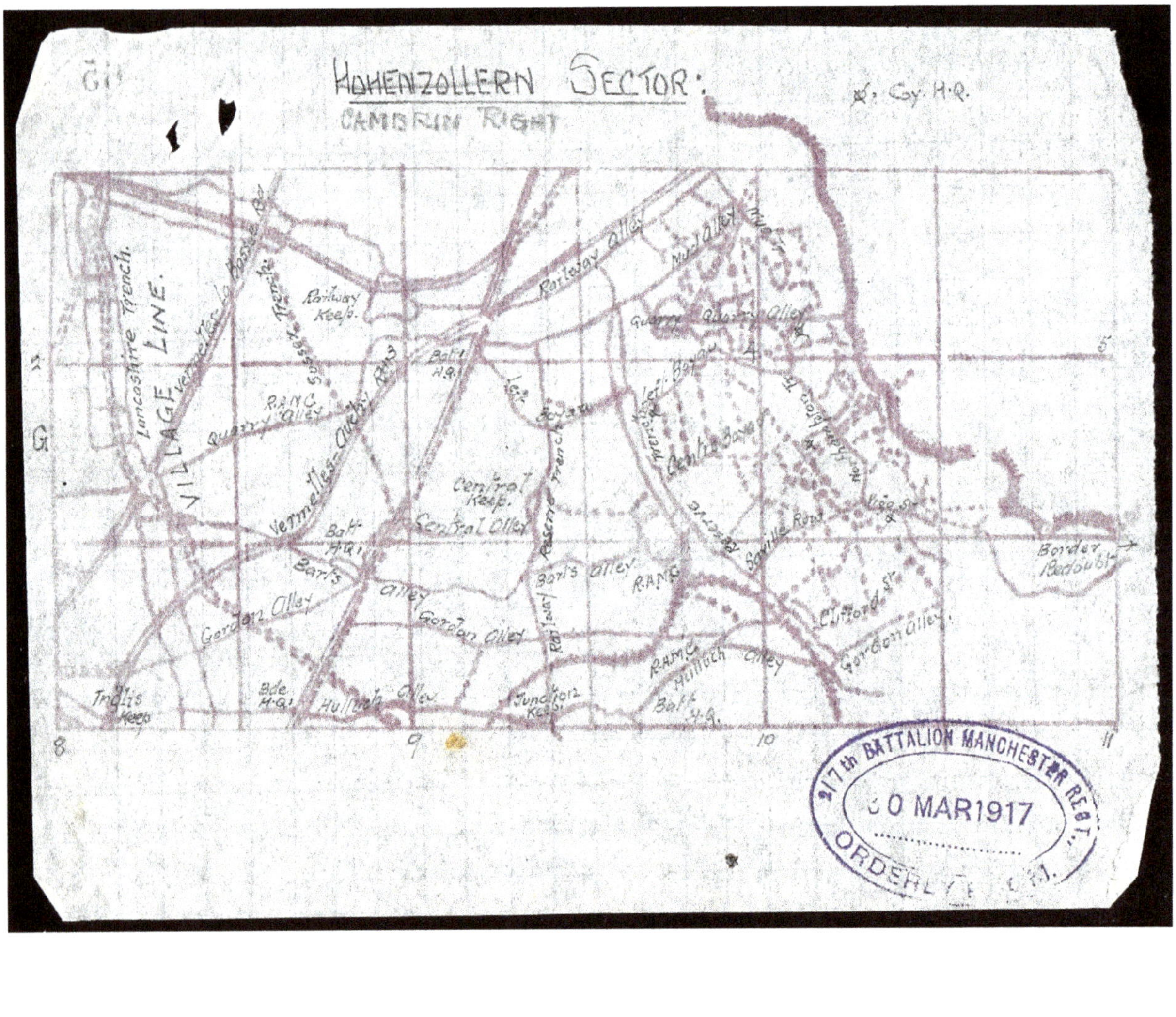

HOHENZOLLERN SECTOR:
CAMBRIN RIGHT
Lancashire Trench
VILLAGE LINE
Railway Keep
Railway Alley
Quarry Alley
R.A.M.C. Alley
Central Keep
Central Alley
Bart's Alley
Gordon Alley
Hulluch Alley
Junction Keep
Bde H.Q.
Border Redoubt
Saville Road
Clifford St.
R.A.M.C.
Batt H.Q.
8
9
10
11
G
5
2/7th BATTALION MANCHESTER REGT.
30 MAR 1917
ORDERLY ROOM

Copy No 11.

2/7th Battalion Manchester Regiment Order No.1.

BETHUNE (Combined Sheet)
Ref.1.40000.

<u>MOVE</u>.	1.	The Battalion will move into Billets at PARADIS to morrow 14th instant.
<u>STARTING POINT</u>.	2.	P 3 b 64. 9-30 a.m.
<u>ORDER OF MARCH</u>.	3.	Headquarters, "A" "B" "C" "D" Companies, Transport. O.C."D" Company will detail 1 Platoon to march in rear of Transport to collect stragglers.
<u>ROUTE</u>.	4.	ST.VENANT - ST.FLORIS - CALONNE SUR LA LYS - LE Pt PACAUT - LE BOUZATEAUX FMe to destination.
<u>DRESS</u>.	5.	F.S.M.O. Steel Helmets will be worn. Greatcoats will be carried in the packs. All articles of kit must be carried either in the pack or haversack and not attached to the equipment. Box respirators and Steel Helmets will be carried by all ranks always on reaching the new billeting area.
<u>BAGGAGE</u>.	6.	Officers Valises will be sent to Q.M.Stores not later than 7-0 a.m.
<u>BLANKETS</u>.	7.	All blankets, rolled in bundles of 20 and labelled will be returned to Q.M.Stores by 7-0 am.
<u>RUNNERS</u>.	8.	Companies will send two runners to Bn.H.Q. on arrival in billets.
	9.	ACKNOWLEDGE.

(Sgd) J.Brown.
Lieut. & A/Adjt,
2/7th Bn. Manchester Regiment.

Issued at 4-30 p.m.

Copy No.1. Retained.
2. 199th Bde.
3. C.O.
4. Adjt.
5. Q.M.
6. T.O.
7. O.C.A.Coy.
8. O.C.B.Coy.
9. O.C.C.Coy.
10. O.C.D.Coy.
11. War Diary.
12. Filed.

Copy No.12

2/7th Battalion Manchester Regiment Order No.2;

BETHUNE (Combined Sheet)
Ref.1.40000.

15.3.17.

MOVE.	1.	The Battalion will move into Billets in the BETHUNE area No.1 to morrow 16.3.17.
STARTING POINT.	2.	PARADIS CHURCH 9-30 a.m. "A" Company will join the column on the march.
ORDER OF MARCH.	3.	Headquarters Company, "B" "C" "D" "A", Transport. O.C."A" Company will detail 1 Platoon to form a Rear Party.
ROUTE.	4.	LES LOBES - LOCON - BETHUNE to destination.
DRESS.	5.	F.S.M.O. Steel Helmets will be carried on the Pack and not worn.
BAGGAGE.	6.	Officers Valises will be collected from Company H.Q. starting "B" Coy.H.Q. 7-30 a.m. O.C."C" Company will detail 1 N.C.O. and 12 men as loading party to report to Q.M.Stores at 7-0 a.m. to load stores.
BLANKETS.	7.	Blankets will be rolled in bundles of 10 and stacked at Company H.Q. by 8-0 a.m. Motor Transport will call for these.
REAR PARTY.	8.	Each Company will detail 1 Section to load blankets and finish cleaning billets. This party will report to 2nd.Lt.Rudd at Bn.H.Q. when the work is completed, and march under him to new billets.
SANITATION.	9.	All latrines must be filled in and billets left clean.
SICK PARADE.	10.	6-30 a.m.
BILLETING PARTY.	11.	This party will report to Capt.Bolton at Bn.H.Q. at 7-0 a.m. to draw bicycles and meet the Staff Captain at E c a 20 at 9-0 a.m.
RUNNERS.	12.	Companies will send two runners to Bn.H.Q. on arrival in new billets.
	13.	ACKNOWLEDGE.

(Sgd) J.Brown,
Lieut. & A/Adjt,
2/7th Bn. Manchester Regiment.

Issued at 10 p.m.

Copy No.1. Retained.
2. 199th Bde.
3. C.O.
4. Adjt.
5. Q.M.
6. T.O.
7. O.C.HMQ.Coy.
8. O.C.A.Coy.
9. O.C.B.Coy.
10. O.C.C.Coy.
11. O.C.D.Coy.
12. War Diary.
13. Filed.
14. M.O.

Copy No.14.

2/7th Battalion Manchester Regiment Order No.3.

18.3.17.

Ref. BETHUNE (Combined Sheet)
1.40000.

RELIEF. 1. The Battalion will relieve the 1st Norfolk Regiment to-morrow in the left CAMBRIN Sector.
Distribution will be as follows:-
"A" Coy. Right Front Line.
"B" " Centre Front Line.
"C" " Left Front Line.
"D" " Support.

GUIDES. 2. Guides will be found (1 per Platoon) at Pt. F 22 c 9.2.

ORDER OF MARCH. 3. Starting Point - Railway Crossing S.E. of BEUVRY Village.
"A" Coy. will leave Starting Point at 8-15 a.m. followed by "B" Coy. H.Q. "C" and "D". respectively at 200 yards interval.
Formations by Companies at F 22 c 9.2., thence Platoons to ANNEQUIN Cross Roads and thence Sections into Line. These formations will be strictly adhered to.
Intervals. 50 yards between Sections. 200 yards between Platoons.

ROUTE. 4. BEUVRY F 22 c 9.2. - ANNEQUIN - CAMBRIN - MAISON ROUGE.

DRESS. 5. F.S.M.O. Steel Helmets will be worn.

FEEDING ARRANGEMENTS. 6. The unexpired portion of the days rations will be carried by the men.
Dixies will be carried up.

STORES. 7. Blankets and Officers Valises will be stacked at the respective by the men.
C.Q.M.S's will be in charge.

TRANSPORT & "B" SECTION, H.Q.COMPANY. 8. These will move to LES QUESNOY under instructions of the Transport Officer, who will arrange billets for the N.C.O's and men concerned.

BICYCLES. 9. The Signalling Officer will arrange for 4 bicycles to be kept at the CAMBRIN Ration Dump, for the use of runners from Bn.H.Q. to 199th Bde.H.Q.

10. ACKNOWLEDGE.

Issued at 10 a.m.

(Sgd) John A.Scholfield,
Capt. & Adjt,
2/7th Bn. Manchester Regiment.

Copy No.1. Retained.
2. 199th Bde.
3. 1st Norfolks.
4. C.O.
5. Adjt.
6. O.C.A.Coy.
7. O.C.B.Coy.
8. O.C.C.Coy.
9. O.C.D.Coy.
10. T.O.
11. Q.M.
12. M.O.
13. O.C.H.Q.Coy.
14. War Diary.
15. Filed.

Copy No.14.

2/7th Battalion Manchester Regiment Order No.4.

22.3.17.

RELIEF. 1. The 2/7th Manch R. will be relieved by the 2/8th Manch R. to-morrow the 23rd inst. Relief to commence at 2-0 p.m.

GUIDES. 2. Guides will be found, 1 Officer per Coy, and 1 N.C.O. per Platoon to meet the incoming Battalion and guide them to the trenches. They will be at the ANNEQUIN CROSS ROADS at 12-30 p.m.

BILLETS. 3. On being relieved the Battalion will proceed into Reserve Billets at ANNEQUIN. Capt. Bolton will meet C.Q.M.S's and Sgt Moult, who will represent H.Q.Coy. at ANNEQUIN CROSS ROADS at 10 a.m.

EXITS FROM TRENCHES. 4. "D" Coy. and 2 Platoons "C" Coy (garrison of Stafford and Mountain Keeps) - BY THE LANE.
"A" and "B" Coys. and 2 Platoons "C" Coy. - BY MAISON ROUGE.

SANITATION. 5. Every effort will be made to leave the trenches in as sanitary a state as possible.

STORES ETC. 6. All trench stores, maps etc. will be handed over and receipts obtained.

BLANKETS. 7. The Transport Officer will arrange to dump Officers Valises and Blankets at respective Coy.H.Q., under charge of Coy.Storemen.

COOKERS. 8. Company Cookers will be parked in as convenient a place as possible.

DETAILS. 9. Coys. may send details, i.e. cooks, servants etc. out of the trenches, prior to relief, but they must be clear by 12 noon.

MEALS. 10. O.C.Coys. will arrange for tea to be issued to the men before leaving the trenches, and for a hot meal upon arrival at ANNEQUIN.
The Q.M. will send up to the dump to night breakfast rations and tea for the middle of the day. The remainder will be issued to Coy.Cooks to morrow under arrangements to be made by the Q.M.

11. Completion of relief to be reported by BAB Code.

12. ACKNOWLEDGE.

(Sgd) John A.Scholfield,
Capt. & Adjt,
2/7th Bn. Manchester Regiment.

Issued at 4-0 p.m.

Copy No.1. Retained.
2. 199 Bde.
3. 2/8th Manch R.
4. C.O.
5. Adjt.
6. O.C.H.Q.Coy.
7. O.C.A.Coy.
8. O.C.B.Coy.
9. O.C.C.Coy.
10. O.C.D.Coy.
11. T.O.
12. Q.M.
13. M.O.
14. War Diary.
15. Filed.

Copy No.1.

2/7th Battalion Manchester Regiment Order No.5.

26.3.17.

Ref.Sheet 36 C.N.W. 1.10000 and
BETHUNE (Combined Sheet) 1.40000.

INTENTION. 1. On March 27th the 66th Division will take over a frontage of one Battalion from the 6th Division.

RELIEF. 2. 2/7th Bn. Manchester Regiment will move into the HOHENZOLLERN SUB-SECTOR to relieve the 9th Leicestershire Regiment.

ORDER OF MARCH. 3. As per attached table.

DISPOSITION. 4. "A" Company - LEFT FIRING LINE.
"B" " - CENTRE FIRING LINE.
"C" " - RIGHT FIRING LINE.
"D" " - IN SUPPORT.

GUIDES. 5. As per attached table.

MAPS ETC. 6. All Defence Schemes, Secret Maps, Aeroplane Photos, Trench Stores etc, will be taken over from the Companies being relieved and receipts given.

DIPOSITION RETURN. 7. On completion of relief, Company Commanders will immediately send in a Disposition Return shewing Company Headquarters, with Map Reference. Completion of Relief will be reported by BAB Code to Bn.H.Q.

SICK PARADE. 8. Sick Parade will be at 7-30 a.m. to-morrow.

BREAKFAST. 9. Breakfast will be arranged under Company arrangements.

BATTALION ARRANGEMENTS. 10. (a) The Transport will deliver Rations to the Railheads for the Companies.
(b) Each Company will ascertain from his "opposite" Company, 9th Leicester, which his Railhead is, and reconnoitre the way from CLARKES KEEP, VERMELLES, to his Company Railhead.
(c) "D" Company will carry all Company Rations from each Railhead to each Company Cookhouse.
(d) GUIDES. Each Company will detail one guide - who has reconnoitred the way - to meet 2nd in Command at CLARKES KEEP, VERMELLES, at 6-30 p.m. to guide trucks to Company Railheads. Each Company will detail two more guides to guide ration carriers of "D" Company from their Railhead to their Company Cookhouse.
(e) Blankets in bundles of 10, Valises and packs (properly labelled) will be stacked at respective Company Headquarters by 7-0 a.m.
(f) Lewis Gun Limbers and Grenade Linber will report to Company H.Q., Grenade Limber to Bn.H.Q.Coy. at 7-0 a.m. and when loaded will proceed in convoy to VERMELLES. Each Company will detail 1 Caretaker for its Limber. Lt.D.Morris will be in charge of this party..

DRESS. 11. Trench Fighting Order.
12. ACKNOWLEDGE.

(Sgd) John A.Scholfield,
Capt. & Adjt,
2/7th Bn. Manchester Regiment.

Issued at 10-45 p.m.

Copy No.1. War Diary. Copy No.2. 199th Bde.
3. O.C.A.Coy. 4. O.C.B.Coy.
5. O.C.C.Coy. 6. O.C.D.Coy.
7. O.C.H.Q.Coy. 8. M.O.
9. T.O. 10. Q.M.

RELIEF OF HOHENZOLLERN SUB-SECTOR
BY THE
2/7th BATTALION MANCHESTER REGIMENT.

Coy.	Leave ANNEQUIN Cross Roads.	Guides. Time.	Guides. Place.	Route.	Relief completed by about.
"C"	8-30 a.m.	9-30 a.m.	CLARKES KEEP G8 a 65.30.	ANNEQUIN VERMELLES ROAD.	
"B"	8-50 a.m.	"	"	"	
"A"	9-10 a.m.	"	"	"	
"D"	9-30 a.m.	"	"	"	
"H.Q."	9-50 a.m.	"	"	"	5-30 p.m.

PARTIES MOVING ALONG THE ANNEQUIN - VERMELLES ROAD WILL DO SO BY PLATOONS AT 500 YARDS INTERVAL.

SECRET. Copy No ......

2/7th Battalion Manchester Regiment Order No. 5.

30.3.17.

1. RELIEF. The Battalion will be relieved in the trenches on the morning of the 31st inst, by the 2/8th Bn. Manch. R. and will proceed into Support.

2. DISPOSITION OF BATTALION IN SUPPORT.

"A" Coy.	VILLAGE LINE, RIGHT SECTOR.
"B" "	RIGHT RESERVE TRENCH.
"C" "	Two Platoons in RAILWAY RESERVE TRENCH. One Platoon in CENTRAL KEEP. One Platoon in LANCASHIRE TRENCH.
"D" "	VILLAGE LINE, LEFT SECTOR.

"D" Company will not move back until 11-30 a.m.

3. ROUTE. In accordance with attached Route Table.

4. HANDING OVER. All trench stores, maps, defence schemes etc. will be handed over to the incoming Unit. Receipts will be obtained.

5. TUNNELS & DUG-OUTS. All Tunnels, dug-outs, cookhouses and latrines, will be left scrupulously clean.

6. DETAILS. Stretcher Bearers, Water duty men, Sanitary men and three Signallers will remain with their Companies, and be rationed by them while in Support.

7. REPORT OF RELIEF. By BAB Code as soon as complete.

8. ACKNOWLEDGE.

John Ashfield Captain,

Issued at 3.50 pm. Adjt, 2/7th Bn. Manchester Regt.

Copy No.1. ~~Retained.~~
2. 199th Bde.
3. C.O.
4. Adjt.
5. 2nd in Command.
6. O.C. "A" Coy.
7. O.C. "B" "
8. O.C. "C" "
9. O.C. "D" "
10. O.C. "H.Q." Coy.
11. O.C. 2/8th Manch R.
12. -do-
13. -do-
14. -do-
15. -do-
16. -do-
17. R.S.M.
18. Q.M.
19. M.O.
20. War Diary.

Time Table and Routes on night 6th [illegible]

Relief of CAMBRAI RIGHT [illegible]

Guides

Relief of	By	By	Time	At	[illegible]
Right [illegible]	[illegible]	[illegible]	[illegible] am	[illegible] [illegible]	[illegible]
[illegible]	[illegible]	[illegible]	[illegible] am	[illegible] [illegible]	[illegible]
Left [illegible]	[illegible]	[illegible]	[illegible] am	[illegible] CORNER	[illegible]
Reserve Trench [illegible]	[illegible]	[illegible]	[illegible] am	[illegible] CORNER	[illegible] [illegible]
Reserve Trench [illegible]	[illegible]	[illegible]	[illegible] am	[illegible]	

Copy

2/7th Bn. Manchester Regt
Daily Intelligence Report No 1
(From 7.0 am 28.3.17 to 7.0 am 29.3.17)

A. OPERATIONS

(i) Artillery

Hohenzollern Test Call at 9.0 pm took two minutes for retaliation. At 4.0 am took 1 min 5 secs. Difficult to obtain retaliation yesterday morning.

(ii) Trench Mortars

L.T.M. active about 11.0 am. Good proportion of shells were duds.

(iii) Machine Guns

Usual traversing along front line parapet at night, otherwise quiet.

(iv) Raids

Nil

B. INTELLIGENCE

(i) Visibility

Good, except early morning when mist hindered observation.

(ii) Patrol

Patrol went out at G.4.b.10.70 at 9.? pm and returned at midnight not having seen any signs of enemy.

Patrol went out from G.4.d.55.00 to reconnoitre ground right of our sector. Went out at 10.30 pm & returned 12.30 am.

Copy

No 1 (cont'd)

(iii) Hostile Artillery

Normal

(iv) Hostile Trench Mortars

Active all day, doing considerable damage to trench works.

(v) New Work
(vi) New Wire } Nil

(vii) Movement & Work

None observed.

(viii) Smoke

Nil.

(ix) General

Boche snipers less active during the night.

Arthur [illegible]
Lieut
I.O.

Copy

2/7th Bn. Manchester Regt.
Daily Intelligence Report
From 7.0 am 29.3.17 to 7.0 am 30.3.17

A. OPERATIONS

(i) Artillery

Our artillery quite active. Good results observed in enemy lines.

(ii) Trench Mortars

Active between 1.0 pm & 7.0 pm.

(iii) Machine Guns

Normal.

(iv) Raids

Nil.

B. INTELLIGENCE

(i) Visibility

Fair. Intermittent rain showers.

(ii) Patrols

The patrol reported in my No 1. that went out from G.4 d 55.60 to reconnoitre ground between our right & next battn. on right returned after having been to GORDON POST then on to a point immediately S. of RUSSIAN SAP. These positions were not occupied at all by battn on our right and the patrol did not establish communication with them.

A patrol of 4 other ranks went out under 2/Lt. Acton to again try to establish communication with the Leicesters on our right. They went out at

Copy

No 2 (Contd)

(i) Patrols (contd)

* 12.30 a.m. The moon was very bright and the patrol was sniped at so returned. Two O.R.s were put out to watch and the remainder went round by VIGO ST., - SAVILLE ROW - GORDON ALLEY to RUSSIAN SAP and met the patrol of the Leicesters who conducted them to Company H.Q. There they obtained the password for the next few days. Patrol returned at 1.0 a.m. RUSSIAN SAP is now held by a Bombing party (of bttn. on our right.)

A second patrol went out under 2/Lt. Hammond at G4d 60.60 and worked NORTH along the wire to post No 4 at G4d 60.70 and saw no signs of enemy patrols.

(ii) Hostile Artillery

About 12.0 noon the H.Q. of right company was shelled, otherwise activity normal

(iii) Hostile T.M.

Very active. Minnies, Rifle Grenades, and Aerial darts very frequent. Retaliation was called for and obtained.

(v) New Work }
(vi) New Wire } None observed.
(vii) Smoke }

(viii) Movement & Work

4 men were seen to enter trench at G4 b 75 62. Visibility only fair

Copy
No 2 (cont)

(X). General.

One enemy periscope broken by sniper, also one hit claimed.

Arthur Empheles[illegible]
Lieut
I.O.

Copy

2/7th Bn. Manchester Regt.

Daily Intelligence Report No 3

(From 7 am 30.3.17 to 7 am 31.3.17)

A. OPERATIONS.

(i) Artillery.

At about 9.45 pm. coloured lights, two green then three red together caused our artillery to start a bombardment of enemy lines which continued for about quarter of an hour. Lights presumably Boche. Otherwise normal.

(ii) Trench Mortars

'Stokes' active in reply to hostile T.M. but not sufficient to silence them.

(iii) Machine Guns

One of our machine guns was busy in the afternoon about 5 o pm against Boche communication trench. Otherwise activity normal.

(iv) Raids

Nil.

B. INTELLIGENCE

(i) Visibility

Good.

(ii) Patrols.

One patrol went out from our right to keep touch with Bn. on right. Moon so bright that trench route taken. Practise patrols were sent out from our reserve line.

Copy

(iii) Hostile Artillery. No 3 (Cont^d)

Fairly active in the afternoon. Two ration carts were shelled but with no result. Probably 77mm guns.

(iv) Hostile T.M.

The Bosche is very active in this sub-sector with Minnies, Rum Jars, Aerial Darts, Rifle Grenades &c. More or less all day he has swept front with them. He again prevented good observation from O.P.

(v) New Work }
(vi) New Wire } no working parties at all observed last night.

(vii) Smoke

Seen at A4 b 9226

(viii) Movement & Work

A working party was observed in the direction of CORONS DE PÉKIN at about A79 c4535

(ix) General

A large cloud of smoke was observed at 9.25 am to rise from direction of A7 b 3080. Possibly an explosion in the works there.

Two copper coated bullets have been found in our reserve trench, evidently from machine guns. Are herewith.

Arthur Smither
Lieut
I.O.

2/7th Bn Manchester Regt
Daily Intelligence Report No 1.
From 7.0 am. 31.3.17 to 3.0 pm. 31.3.17
Relief

A. OPERATIONS.

(i) Artillery
Normal

(ii) Trench Mortars
Our "Stokes" were active in morning.

(iii) Machine Guns
Quiet

(iiii) Raids
Nil

B. INTELLIGENCE

(i) Visibility
Good.

(ii) Patrols
Nil

(iii) Hostile artillery
Normal

(iiii) Hostile T. M.
Active with Minnies and Aerial Darts along NORTHAMPTON TRENCH.

(v) New work } None observed
(vi) New wire }

(vii) Smoke
Seen at A.4.b 92.26

(viii) Movement & work
None reported

603

No 4 (contd)

(x) General.

We put over 110 Rifle Grenades in the morning between 6 am & 7 am. which were observed to have obtained good results.

Several Gas shells fell in the lines of our left firing line company. Particulars will be sent later. Respirators were worn.

Arthur Smithies
Lieut.
I.O.

2/5th Bn Manchester Regt
Supplement to
Daily Intelligence Report No 4
From 7.0 am 31.3.17 to 3.0 pm 4.3.17

(ix) General

One gas shell was seen to fall at a point about 9 c b 05.40 (20 yds behind front line), at about 12.0 noon. Gas was seen to rise at once after the explosion and could be smelt. Respirators were used for about 10 to 15 minutes.

A small flag was observed earlier in the morning sticking on German parapet

Arthur Smith
Lieut
I.O.

War Diary

of

2/4 Bn The Manchester Regt.

from March 6th to March 31st

1917.

Volume 1.

Appendix.

A. T.P.R's.
B. Operation Orders.
C. Casualty returns
D. Maps.

Appendix A

T. P. R's.

SECRET

Time Table and Routes on March 31st — RELIEF DAY.

Relief of CAMBRIN RIGHT – 2/4th MANCHESTERS BY 2/8th MANCHESTERS.

– GUIDES –

RELIEF OF	COY.	BY.	TIME	AT.	ROUTE.	COMPLETE BY.
LEFT FIRING LINE.	"A" COY 2/4.	"D" COY 2/8.	9-0 AM.	JUNCTION RESERVE & QUARRY ALLEY.	Rt RESERVE TRENCH – QUARRY ALLEY.	2-0 P.M.
CENTRE FIRING LINE.	"B" COY. 2/4.	"A" COY 2/8.	9-0 A.M.	" " LANCASHIRE TR. & QUARRY ALLEY (WINDY CORNER)	QUARRY ALLEY. RESERVE TR. LEFT BOYAU.	2-0 P.M.
RIGHT FIRING LINE.	"C" COY. 2/4.	"C" COY 2/8	9-0. A.M.	SAVILLE ROW & RESERVE TRS.	SAVILLE ROW.	2-0. P.M.
RIGHT SUPPORT LINE	"C" COY 2/7	"B" COY 2/8	10-0. A.M.	LANCASHIRE TRENCH & QUARRY ALLEY.	QUARRY ALLEY & RESERVE TR	2-0. P.M.
LEFT SUPPORT LINE	"D" COY 2/4.	"B" COY 2/4.	9-0 A.M.		LEFT BOYAU.	2-0. P.M.

NOTE

(1) Situation of H.Q. Coy 2/4th Bn. MAN. R. will be ANNEQUIN FOSSE

(2) Companies of the 2/8th Bn. MAN. R. will each leave a representative [illegible] to hand over SUPPORT LINE to Companies of the 2/4th Bn MAN. R.

Transport Return

22nd Bn. Manchester Regiment

[illegible] Transport

[illegible]	Nil	Nil

[illegible] Lieut Colonel

Commanding 22nd Bn [illegible]

H.Q.

23/3/17

Appendix "B"

Operation Orders.

APPENDIX "B"

Appendix "C".

Casualty Returns.

2/7th Battalion Manchester Regiment.

Casualties during the period
6.3.17 to 31.3.17.

	KILLED.		WOUNDED.		ACCIDENTLY WOUNDED.		
	Offrs.	O.R.	Offrs.	O.R.	Offrs.	O.R.	
20.3.17.	-	-	-	2	-	-	
21.3.17.	-	3	-	2	-	1	
23.3.17.	-	-	-	1	-	-	
28.3.17.	-	1	-	4	-	1	(~~accident~~ (
29.3.17.	-	1	-	-	-	-	
30.3.17.	-	1	-	5	-	-	
31.3.17.	-	-	-	1	-	-	

Captain,
Adjt, 2/7th Bn. Manchester Regt.

In the Field,
1.4.17.

Appendix "D"

Maps.

66

— CONFIDENTIAL —

WAR DIARY

OF Vol 2

2/7th Bn THE MANCHESTER Regt

FROM. APRIL 1st 1917 TO. APRIL 30th 1917

— VOLUME 2. —

Instructions regarding War Diaries and Intelligence Summaries are contained in F. S. Regs., Part II. and the Staff Manual respectively. Title Pages will be prepared in manuscript.

WAR DIARY
~~or~~ and
INTELLIGENCE SUMMARY
(Erase heading not required.)

Army Form C. 2118.

Place	Date	Hour	Summary of Events and Information	Remarks and references to Appendices
ANNEQUIN	1-4-17	2.30 pm	1 man wounded accidentally	[illegible]
ANNEQUIN	3.4.17	6.30 pm	Order No 7 issued for relief of 2/8 Man by 2/7 Manchester Regiment	
"	"	8.0 pm	1 man wounded	[illegible]
CAMBRIN RIGHT	4.4.17		1 man killed	[illegible]
" "	5.4.17		2 men wounded	[illegible]
" "	6.4.17		1 man wounded	
" "	7.4.17		Captain G. A. Allan wounded (slightly)	[illegible]
" "	......	5-45 pm	Order No 8 issued for relief of 2/7 Manchesters by 2/8 Manchesters	[illegible]
" "	8.4.17	9 am	1 man wounded	[illegible]
NOYELLES	8.4.17 to 12.4.17		Bn in Brigade Reserve at NOYELLES	[illegible]
" "	11.4.17	11 pm	1 man wounded (on working party)	[illegible]
" "	11.4.17	4.30 pm	Order No 9 issued for relief of 2/8 Manchesters by 2/7 Manchesters	[illegible]
CAMBRIN RIGHT	12.4.17		4 OR wounded	[illegible]
	13.4.17		3 OR wounded 1 OR killed	
	14.4.17		2 OR killed 2/Lt J.W.G. Claton wounded 1 OR wounded	[illegible]
	15.4.17	6 pm	Order No 10 issued for relief of 2/7 Manchesters by 2/8 Manchesters	[illegible]
VILLAGE LINE	16.4.17	am	2 OR killed 1 OR wounded	[illegible]
	19.4.17		Bn in SUPPORT in VILLAGE LINE Bn H.Q FOSSE HOUSE	[illegible]
	19.4.17	5-15 pm	Order No 11 issued for relief of 2/8 Manchesters by 2/7 M/c in CAMBRIN RIGHT	[illegible]
CAMBRIN RIGHT	21.4.17		1 OR killed	[illegible]

Instructions regarding War Diaries and Intelligence Summaries are contained in F. S. Regs., Part II. and the Staff Manual respectively. Title Pages will be prepared in manuscript.

WAR DIARY ~~or~~ and INTELLIGENCE SUMMARY

(Erase heading not required.)

Army Form C. 2118.

Place	Date	Hour	Summary of Events and Information	Remarks and references to Appendices
CAMBRIN RIGHT	22/4/17		3 OR killed 1 OR wounded	[illegible]
	23/4/17		1 OR killed 1 OR wounded 1 OR died of wounds	[illegible]
	23/4/17	4-15pm	Order Number 12 issued for relief. Cancelled and Bn to stay in line another 4 days	[illegible]
	24/4/17		1 OR wounded	
	25/4/17		1 OR killed 3 OR wounded	[illegible]
VILLAGE LINE	27/4/17	4pm	Order Number 13 issued for relief of Bn by 2/5 M/c Bn goes into VILLAGE LINE	[illegible]
	29/4/17		2nd Lieut G. W. C. Cowsill gassed (wounded)	[illegible]
	30/4/17		1 OR wounded.	

[signature] Lieut Colonel

Commanding 2/7 Bn Manchester Regt

30/4/17

SECRET

Copy No ..13.....

2/7th Battalion Manchester Regiment Order No.7.

3.4.17.

1. The Battalion will relieve the 2/8th Manch. R. in CAMBRIN RIGHT (late HOHENZOLLERN) trenches to-morrow 4.4.17.

2. Companies will take up positions as follows:-
   "C" Coy. RIGHT FIRING LINE.
   "B" " CENTRE FIRING LINE.
   "D" " LEFT FIRING LINE.
   "A" " SUPPORT - RESERVE TRENCH (Right Sector).

3. "A" Coy. will supply 1 Bombing Squad (8 Other Ranks) to be attached to "B" Coy. for duty and rations during this tour. A Company of the 2/6th Manch R. in RAILWAY RESERVE Trench will supply 1 Bombing Squad (8 Other Ranks) to be attached to "C" Coy. for duty and rations.

4. Snipers will be under the orders of their respective Coys.

5. Ration arrangements as for last tour. "A" Coy. will carry rations.

6. Guides. Companies will each leave a Coy. representative, a responsible N.C.O. as Coy. guide as follows:-
   "D" Coy. at TOURBIERE REDOUBT.
   "A" " at JUNCTION OF VILLAGE LINE AND RAILWAY - RUINED HOUSE.
   "B" " at JUNCTION OF CUT TO QUARRY ALLEY.
   "C" " at JUNCTION OF CUT TO QUARRY ALLEY.
   "B" and "C" Coys. will leave Platoon representatives in addition, to hand over Platoon positions.

7. No parties larger than Platoons at 300 yards interval will move for relief. In exposed places, or where, it is essential, through lack of communication trenches, to move up over the open, move will be by Sections only.

8. Companies who require Transport to take stores, blankets etc. to Q.M.Stores will arrange direct with the Transport Officer.

9. Completion of relief by BAB Code.

10. ACKNOWLEDGE.

Issued at 6-30pm

John Aldersley(?) Captain,
Adjt, 2/7th Bn. Manchester Regt.

Copy No.1. 199th Bde.
2. 2/8th Manch R.
3. 2/6th " "
4. O.C.H.Q.Coy.
5. O.C.A.Coy.
6. O.C.B.Coy.
7. O.C.C.Coy.
8. O.C.D.Coy.
9. T.O.& Q.M.
10. M.O.
11. R.S.M.
12. War Diary.
13. " "
14. " "
15. Filed.

SECRET. Copy No 16

2/7th Battalion Manchester Regiment Order No.8.

7.4.17.

1. The Battalion will be relieved by the 2/5th Manch R. in CAMERIN RIGHT Trench System to-morrow 8.4.17.

2. The Battalion will go into Brigade Reserve at NOYELLES.

3. Relief will be as per attached route table.

4. No Parties larger than Platoons at 500 yards interval will move on Relief. In exposed places, or where it is essential, through lack of communication trenches, to move out over the open, move will be by Sections only.

5. Trench Stores. A receipt will be obtained for the trench stores, maps, aeroplane photographs etc, handed over to the incoming Battalion, and copies of these receipts will be forwarded to Battalion Headquarters by 8 p.m. on the day of relief.

6. Stores. Evacuation of dixies, mess boxes, surplus kit etc. will be in accordance with J.E.R./1, issued to-day. The Quarter-Master will arrange for the C.Q.M.S's to meet their Companies on arrival at NOYELLES in order to guide them to their billet area. He will also arrange to dump at respective Company Headquarters blankets (2 per man) valises and packs.

7. SANITATION. All cookhouses, dug-outs, latrines and trenches will be left scrupulously clean.

8. Completion of relief will be reported by BAB Code.

9. ACKNOWLEDGE.

Issued at 5.45pm

[signature]
Captain,
Adjt, 2/7th Bn. Manchester Regiment.

Copy No. 1.. 199th Bde.
2. 2/5th Manch R.
3. 2/6th Manch R.
4. 2/8th Manch R.
5. O.C.H.Q.Coy.
6. O.C.A.Coy.
7. O.C.B.Coy.
8. O.C.C.Coy.
9. O.C.D.Coy.
10. R.S.M.
11. M.O.
12. Q.M.
13. T.O.
14. War Diary.
15. " "
16. " "
17. Filed.

Relief of CAMBRIN RIGHT 2/7th Manc. R. by 2/8th Manc. R. on 8/4/17

Time Table and Routes on 8/4/17. Relief Day.

Relief of	Coy	By	Time	At	Route	Relief Complete By.
Right Firing Line	C Coy 2/7th	B Coy 2/8th	10-30 am	INGLIS KEEP HULLOCH ALLEY	HULLOCH ALLEY SAVILLE ROW.	
Centre Firing Line	B Coy 2/7th	A Coy 2/8th	10-30 am	WINDY CORNER	QUARRY. ALLEY LEFT. BOYEU	
Left Firing Line	D Coy 2/7th	D Coy 2/8th	11-0 am	WINDY CORNER	QUARRY. ALLEY QUARRY TUNNEL	
Right Reserve.	A Coy 2/7th	C Coy 2/8th	11-0 am.	INGLIS KEEP HULLOCH ALLEY.	HULLOCH ALLEY RESERVE TRENCH	4 p.m.

The relief of 2 Coys 2/6th Manc. R. in Reserve Trench (Left) and Railway Reserve Trench by 2 Coy of 2/6th Manch. R. will be complete and Companies clear by 10-30 am

Time Table of Routes on April 12th Relief Day

Relief of CAMBRIN RIGHT. – 2/8th Bn. R. War. Rif. by 2/7th Bn. R. War. Rif.

– GUIDES –

Relief of	Coy	By	Time	R.V.	Routes	Relief Complete By
LEFT. FIRING LINE	D. 2/8th	D. 2/7th	10-30 AM.	WINDY CORNER	QUARRY ALLEY	
CENTRE FIRING LINE	A. 2/8th	A. 2/7th	11-0 AM.	WINDY CORNER.	QUARRY ALLEY RESERVE TRENCH LEFT BOYAU	
RIGHT FIRING LINE	B. 2/8th	C. 2/7th	10-30 AM.	INGLIS KEEP.	HULLOCK ALLEY SAVILLE ROW HULLOCK ALLEY	
SUPPORT (RIGHT RESERVE)	C. 2/8th	B. 2/7th	11-0 AM.	INGLIS KEEP.	RESERVE TRENCH	4.P.M.

SECRET. Copy No ..10....

2/7th Battalion Manchester Regiment Order No.2.

11.4.17.

1. The Battalion will relieve the 2/8th Manch R. in CAMERIN RIGHT trenches to-morrow 12.4.17.

2. Companies will take up positions as follows:-
"C" Coy. RIGHT FIRING LINE.
"A" " CENTRE FIRING LINE.
"D" " LEFT FIRING LINE.
"B" " SUPPORT - RESERVE TRENCH (Right Sector)

3. "B" Coy. will detail 1 Bombing Squad of 8 Other Ranks to report to O.C."A" Coy. at 8 a.m. 12.4.17, and also will detail the same size of squad to report to O.C."C" Coy. at 7 p.m. 12.4.17, in the Line. These squads will be attached to "A" Coy. and "C" Coy. respectively for duty and rations during this tour.

4. Snipers will be under the orders of their respective Coys.

5. Ration arrangements as for last tour, "B" Coy. will carry rations.

6. (a) Packs, blankets, Officers valises and surplus stores, kit etc, will be dumped outside respective Coy. H.Q. by 8 am.
(b) The Quarter-Master will arrange for the 4 Lewis Gun Carts, mess cart, and a limber for Headquarters to report at NOYELLES at 8 a.m.

7. No parties larger than Platoons at 300 yards interval will move for relief. In exposed places, or where, it is essential, through lack of communication trenches, to move up over the open, move will be by Sections only.

8. Completion of relief by BAB Code.

9. ACKNOWLEDGE.

Issued at 4-30pm

John Schofield Captain,
Adjt, 2/7th Bn. Manchester Regt.

Copy No.1. 199th Bde.
2. O.C.H.Q.Coy.
3. O.C.A.Coy.
4. O.C.B.Coy.
5. O.C.C.Coy.
6. O.C.D.Coy.
7. T.O. & Q.M.
8. M.O.
9. R.S.M.
10. War Diary.
11. " "
12. " "
13. Filed.

SECRET. Copy No ..13.....

2/7th Battalion Manchester Regiment Order No.10.

15.4.17.

1. The Battalion will be relieved by the 2/8th Manch R. in CAMBRIN RIGHT SECTOR to-morrow 16.4.17. The Battalion will go into Support.

2. Relief as per attached Route Table.

3. New Dispositions of Companies in Support:-

"A" Coy. RESERVE TRENCH (LEFT SECTOR).
"B" " VILLAGE LINE (RIGHT SECTOR).
"C" " BILLETS IN LA BASSEE ROAD (LA TOURBIERE).
"D" " (less 1 Platoon) to RAILWAY RESERVE TRENCH AND CENTRAL KEEP.
" " 1 Platoon to RESERVE TRENCH (LEFT SECTOR) to report to O.C."A" Coy.
Headquarters to FOSSE HOUSE.

4. No parties larger than Platoons at 300 yards distance will move in relief. In exposed places where it is necessary, owing to lack of communication trenches, to move in the open, movement will be by Sections only.

5. Transport. All arrangements for Transport will be made direct with the Quarter-Master.

6. Rations. As per standing orders issued. 31/3/17

7. Trench Stores. A receipt will be taken for Trench Stores, maps, post boards etc. handed over.

8. Sanitation. All dug-outs, cookhouses, latrines etc. to be left scrupulously clean.

9. Completion of Relief to be reported by BAB II Code.

10. ACKNOWLEDGE.

Issued at 6 pm .... [signature]
Captain,
Adjt, 2/7th Bn.Manchester Regt.

Copy No.1. Retained.
2. 199th Bde.
3. 2/6th Manch R.
4. O.C.H.Q.Coy.
5. O.C.A.Coy.
6. O.C.B.Coy.
7. O.C.C.Coy.
8. O.C.D.Coy.
9. M.O.
10. Q.M.& T.O.
11. R.S.M.
12. War Diary.
13. " "
14. " "
15. " "

Secret

AFTER ORDER.

(1) Owing to an Order issued by 199th Bde since the issue of Order No.10 the following alterations have "of necessity" been made.

In para 3 for "A" Coy. read "C" Coy.
" " " " "C" " " "A" " IN THE VILLAGE LINE (LEFT)

(2) No traffic of any description must take place on the road VERMELLES - ANNEQUIN to-morrow.
"A" & "B" Companies will go to their Support positions by RAILWAY ALLEY (down) but must not been in RAILWAY ALLEY until after 1-0.p.m.

(3) The R.S.M. will post Patrols at WINDY CORNER and CLARKES KEEP and the junction of VERMELLES - NOYELLES and VERMELLES - ANNEQUIN road.

(4) All Transport will use the VERMELLES - SAILLY LABOURSE ROAD.

John Oldfield
Captain.
Adjt. 2/7th Bn.Manchester Regiment

Bn.H.Q.
15.4.17.

Relief Day. 16/4/17.

(1) Centre Firing Line. 'A' Coy 2/7th relieved by 'A' Coy 2/8th
(2) Right Reserve Trench. B Coy 2/7th " " D Coy 2/8th

Guides WINDY CORNER (1) 9-30 am
(2) 10-0 am

(3) Right Firing Line. C Coy 2/7th relieved by B Coy 2/8th
(4) Left Firing Line D Coy 2/7th " C Coy 2/8th

(3) and (4) to be completed by 9-15 am.

(5) Exits in After Order.

(Sgd) John A. Scholfield Captain
Adjt, 2/7th Bn. Manchester Regt.

Bn HQ
15/4/17.

Copy No ...14...

2/7th Battalion Manchester Regiment Order No.11.

19.3.17.

1. RELIEF. The Battalion will relieve the 2/8th Manch R. in the CAMBRIN RIGHT sector to-morrow, the 20th instant.

2. DISPOSITION OF COMPANIES.
Right Firing Line - "B" Coy.
Centre " " - "D" "
Left " " - "A" "
Right Reserve Trench - "C" "
O.C."C" Coy. will detail the following parties to the Firing Line Companies as follows:-
1 Bombing Squad (1 NCO & 8 O.R.) will report to O.C."B" Coy. at 7 pm.
1 " " (1 " " 8 ") " " " " O.C."D" Coy. at 7 pm.
2 Lewis Guns, each with a team of 1 N.C.O. and 6 men will report to O.C."A" Coy. at 10 a.m. in the Line.

3. RATIONS. As usual. "C" Coy. will provide the ration parties.

4. TRANSPORT. O's C.Coys. will arrange what Transport they require. The Transport Officer will arrange for two Limbers, Mess Cart and Maltese Cart to be at FORGE HOUSE at 8-30 a.m. O.C."H.Q" Coy. will detail unloading parties to conduct the convoy to CLARKS KEEP where stores will be dumped until night-fall, when they will be taken up with the rations.

5. MOVEMENT. In future no movement by day over the top will take place East of the following line:-
WATER TOWER (G 8 d 2.5) - VILLAGE LINE - MAISON ROUGE - BARLAY STREET (exclusive).

6. ORDER OF MOVE.
"D" Coy. RAILWAY RESERVE TRENCH, SAVILLE ROW, to be complete by 8-45 am.
"C" " RESERVE TRENCH, to be complete by 9-15 a.m.
"B" " RAILWAY ALLEY, THE CUT, QUARRY ALLEY, RESERVE TRENCH, LEFT BOYAU, to move from junction of RAILWAY ALLEY AND VILLAGE LINE at 8-30 a.m.
"A" " VILLAGE LINE, RAILWAY ALLEY, QUARRY ALLEY, to move from junction of RAILWAY ALLEY and VILLAGE LINE at 9 a.m.
"H.Q"" RAILWAY ALLEY, THE CUT, CANNON STREET, to move from junction of RAILWAY ALLEY and VILLAGE LINE at 9-30 a.m.

7. STORES. No stores of any description will be taken up to the Line from CLARKS KEEP until night-fall.

8. TRENCH STORES. Receipts will be given for all trench stores, maps etc. taken over, and copies forwarded to Battalion Headquarters by 8 p.m. 20.3.17.

9. SANITATION. All trenches, dug-outs, latrines, cookhouses etc. will be handed over in a scrupulously clean condition.

10. Completion of Relief will be reported immediately by BAB XI Code.

11. ACKNOWLEDGE.

Issued at .5.15.pm

John [illegible] Captain,
Adjt, 2/7th Bn. Manchester Regt.

Copy No.1. Retained.	No.2. 198th Bde.	No.3. 2/5th Manch R.
4. 2/6th Manch R.	5. 2/8th Manch R.	6. ~~[illegible]~~
7. O.C.A.Coy.	8. O.C.B.Coy.	9. O.C.H.Q.Coy.
10. O.C.D.Coy.	11. Q.M.& T.O.	12. O.C.C.Coy. M.O.
13. R.S.M.	14. War Diary.	15. War Diary.
16. War Diary.	17. Filed.	

SECRET.

Copy No ...15...

2/7th Battalion Manchester Regiment Order No.14.

23.4.17.

1. The Battalion will be relieved by the 2/6th Manch R. in CAMBRIN RIGHT Trench System to-morrow 24.4.17.

2. The Battalion will go into Brigade Reserve at NOYELLES.

3. Route. "C" "D" & "H.Q" Coys. by way of VILLAGE ALLEY and ENGLISH KEEP, thence by Sections to NOYELLES.
"A" & "B" Coys. by way of QUARRY ALLEY and WINDY CORNER, thence by Sections to NOYELLES.
Relief to be complete by 12 noon.

4. No parties larger than Platoons at 200 yards interval will move on Relief. In exposed places, or where it is essential, through lack of communication trenches, to move out over the open, move will be by Sections only.

5. Trench Stores. A receipt will be obtained for the Trench Stores, Maps, Aeroplane Photographs etc. handed over to the incoming Battalion, and copies of these receipts will be forwarded to Battalion Headquarters by 8 p.m. on the day of Relief.

6. Stores. Evacuation of Mess boxes, surplus kit etc. will be in accordance with JAR/1, issued on 7.4.17. The Quarter-Master will arrange for the C.Q.M.S's to meet their Companies on arrival at NOYELLES in order to guide them to their billet area. He will also arrange to dump at respective Company Headquarters Blankets (2 per man), valises and packs. Each Company will hand over to the incoming Unit all dixies taken over on last Relief.

7. Sanitation. All cookhouses, dug-outs, latrines and trenches will be left scrupulously clean.

8. Gum Boots. All gum boots will be thoroughly cleaned and the tops turned down, and dumped at Company Headquarters by 8 a.m. on 24.4.17. The Transport Officer will arrange for necessary Transport to collect these at the time stated, and return them to Store.

9. Completion of Relief will be reported by BAB II Code.

10. ACKNOWLEDGE.

Issued at ..4.15 p.m.

(Sgd) John A.Scholfield, Captain,
Adjt, 2/7th Bn. Manchester Regiment.

Copy No.1. Retained.
2. 199th Bde.
3. 2/6th Manch R.
4. 2/5th " "
5. 2/8th " "
6. O.C.H.Q.Coy.
7. O.C.A.Coy.
8. O.C.B.Coy.
9. O.C.C.Coy.
10. O.C.D.Coy.
11. M.G.O.
12. M.O.
13. Q.M.& T.O.
14. War Diary.
15. " "
16. " "
17. Filed.

SECRET. Copy No. 14.

2/7th Battalion Manchester Regiment Order No.12.

[illegible].4.17.

1. The Battalion will be relieved by the 2/5th Manch R. to-morrow [illegible], and will go into Support.

2. Disposition of Companies in Support Line:-
   - "A" Coy. LEFT RESERVE TRENCH.
   - "B" " RIGHT RESERVE TRENCH.
   - "C" " LEFT VILLAGE LINE (LA TO[illegible])
   - "D" " RIGHT VILLAGE LINE.

3. Order of Move. In accordance with attached Time Table.

4. Kits etc. O's C.Coys. will arrange with the Quarter-Master for blankets, valises etc. to be brought up. The Transport Officer will dump the valises of Headquarters Officers at [illegible] HOUSE.

5. STRAGGLING. Attention is again called to orders issued re straggling. There will be an interval of at least [illegible] an hour between Companies and at least 500 yards between Platoons.
No parties larger than Platoons at 500 yards interval will move on Relief. In exposed places, or where it is essential, through lack of communication trenches, to move out over the open, move will be by Sections only.

6. Dixies and Lewis Gun ammunition will be taken back by Companies.

7. Cleanliness. O's C.Coys. are again warned that the men must be shaved daily and clean in the Support Line.

8. Inspection. The General Officer Commanding the Division will probably be round the CAMBRIN RIGHT Sector to-morrow.

9. Trench Stores. A receipt will be obtained for all trench stores, maps etc. handed over to the incoming Battalion, and copies of these receipts will be forwarded to Battalion Headquarters by 8 p.m. on the day of Relief.

10. Sanitation. All cookhouses, dug-outs, latrines and trenches will be left scrupulously clean.

11. Completion of Relief will be immediately reported by BAB II Code.

12. ACKNOWLEDGE.

Issued at [illegible]

Captain,
Adjt, 2/7th Bn. Manchester Regiment.

Copy No.1. Retained.
2. 199th Bde.
3. 2/5th Manch R.
4. 2/6th " "
5. O.C.H.Q.Coy.
6. O.C.A.Coy.
7. O.C.B.Coy.
8. O.C.C.Coy.
9. O.C.D.Coy.
10. M.O.
11. Q.M.& T.O.
12. R.S.M.
13. War Diary.
14. " "
15. " "
16. Filed.

66

— CONFIDENTIAL —

Vol 3

WAR DIARY

— OF —

2/7th Bn. THE MANCHESTER REGT.

FROM: MAY 1st 1917. TO: MAY 31st 1917.

— VOLUME 3 —

23·4·17 = RELIEF DAY

RELIEF OF.	COY.	BY COY 2/5TH	GUIDES. AT	GUIDES. TIME	RELIEF COMPLETED BY.
RIGHT FIRING LINE.	C	D	NIL		9-30 AM
CENTRE FIRING LINE.	B	D	NIL		9-30 AM
LEFT FIRING LINE	A	C	WINDY CORNER	10-45 AM	2-0 PM
RIGHT RESERVE TR.	D	A	WINDY CORNER	11-15 AM.	2-0 PM

"C" COY. 2/7TH WILL BE CLEAR OF WINDY CORNER BY. 10-15 AM

Instructions regarding War Diaries and Intelligence Summaries are contained in F. S. Regs., Part II. and the Staff Manual respectively. Title Pages will be prepared in manuscript.

WAR DIARY
or
INTELLIGENCE SUMMARY
(Erase heading not required.)

Army Form C. 2118.

Place	Date	Hour	Summary of Events and Information	Remarks and references to Appendices
FOSSE HOUSE	1/5/17	8 PM	Order No 14 issued for relief of 2/6 Bn Man Regt in CAMBRAIN LEFT by 2/7 Bn Man Regt	JHS
CAMBRAIN LEFT	2/5/17	-	1 OR killed	JHS
" "	3/5/17	-	1 OR died of wounds 1 OR killed	JHS
" "	4/5/17		1 OR wounded	JHS
" "	5/5/17	.	2 OR killed 5 OR wounded	JHS
" "	5/5/17	5-30PM	Order No 15 issued for relief of 2/7 Bn Man Regt by 2/6 Bn Man Regt 2/7 go into Reserve at NOYELLES	JHS
" "	6/5/17		2 OR killed	JHS
NOYELLES	8/5/17		1 OR wounded	JHS
" "	11/5/17	8-30PM	Order No 16 issued for relief of 2/8 Bn Man Regt by 2/7 Bn Man Regt in CAMBRAIN RIGHT	JHS
~~ditto~~ "	9/5/17		REINFORCEMENTS 27 OR received	JHS
CAMBRAIN RIGHT	14/5/17		Missing on patrol 4 OR.	JHS
" "	15/5/17		2 OR killed	JHS
" "	16/5/17		3 OR wounded (accidentally) in action against the enemy.	JHS
" "	17/5/17		2 OR wounded	JHS
" "	17/5/17	4-30PM	Order No 17 issued for relief of 2/7 Bn Man Regt by 2/8 Bn Man Regt 2/7th goes into Support with HQ at ANNEQUIN	JHS
ANNEQUIN	23/5/17		1 OR killed (aeroplane bomb) Bn to be in SUPPORT 9 days	JHS
" "	24/5/17		Capt J. A. Allan - wounded (accidentally)	JHS
" "	26/5/17	1-30PM	Order No 18 issued for relief of 2/8 Bn Man Regt by 2/7th Bn Man Regt. Bn to be in 9 days	JHS
CAMBRAIN RIGHT	27/5/17 to 31/5/17		Ordinary Trench warfare Casualties 4 OR killed 6 OR wounded	

W Horrocks Lieut-Colonel
Commanding 2/7 Bn Manchester Regiment

SECRET. Copy No. 14.....

2/7th Battalion Manchester Regiment Order No.19.

4.5.17.

RELIEF. The Battalion will be relieved to-morrow by the 2/8th Manch R. and will go into Reserve at NOYELLES.

2. ROUTE. In accordance with attached Route Table.

3. HANDING OVER. Companies will obtain a receipt for all Trench Stores, Maps, Documents, etc. handed over, and will forward to the Adjutant, by 4-0 a.m. on 5.5.17, a list of Documents handed over.
Attention is called to this office No.20/26.

4. EVACUATION OF STORES. Kits, Mess Baskets, Dixies, etc. will be sent down to-night as far as possible.
O's C.Coys. will arrange to keep over until to-morrow the very minimum which will enable them to carry on.

5. TRANSPORT ARRANGEMENTS. The Transport Officer will arrange to park Limbers containing stores sent down to-night in his Lines until the morning. They will then be taken to NOYELLES together with Officers Valises, Packs etc. and one Blanket per man, and dumped under the charge of the C.Q.M.S's.
He will bring Rations at night to NOYELLES and will continue with the empty Limbers to VERMELLES, where he will load with Lewis Guns, Mess Baskets, etc. and return to Company Lines at NOYELLES.

6. WORK DONE. O's C.Coys. will render a return shewing work done during tour by 10-0 p.m. to-night.

7. NIGHT RELIEF. It must be pointed out to all ranks that the great secret of the success of a night relief is quietness. There must be no noise or shouting and special care must be paid to the fitting of equipment.

8. SANITATION. All trenches, dug_outs, latrines, etc. will be left scrupulously clean, and fires in Cookhouses burning.

9. Completion of Relief will be immediately reported by BAB II Code.

10. ACKNOWLEDGE.

Issued at 10.15 pm

(sgd) John A.Scholfield, Captain,
Adjutant,
2/7th Bn. Manchester Regt.

Copy No.1. Retained.
2. 2/5th Manch R.
3. 2/6th " "
4. 2/8th " "
5 to 9. Coys.
10. T.O.
11. Q.M.
12. M.O.
13. R.S.M.
14 to 16. War Diary.
17. Filed.
18. "A" Coy, 2/8th Manch R.
19. "B" " " " "

SECRET. Copy No 12

8/7th Battalion Manchester Regiment Order No.16.

11.5.17.

1. RELIEF. The Battalion will relieve the 2/8th Manch R. in the CAMBRIN RIGHT Sector to-morrow 12th instant.

2. ROUTE. Relief will be carried out in accordance with attached route table.

3. MARCH DISCIPLINE. Trenches will be used wherever they exist. If road laid down is under shell fire, another road or open fields should be used.

4. USE OF COVER. Officers or N.C.O's in charge of Parties or Platoons will be especially careful to avoid being seen by the enemy. Should hostile aeroplanes appear Parties should leave the road and lie down. It is particularly important that this relief should not be suspected by the enemy.

5. STORES ETC. Officers valises, blankets, packs (with greatcoats inside) will be packed and dumped outside respective Company Headquarters by 7-45 a.m. The Transport Officer will arrange for limbers to call for these at 8-0 a.m. and convey them to the Quarter-Masters Stores.
Officers trench kit, dixies etc. which are not actually carried up will be dumped outside Company Headquarters and a man put in charge. The Transport Officer will arrange for the Company ration limbers to take these things up, on the way to CLARKS KEEP at night.

6. CONVALESCENT HOME. No.275067.Sgt Bond W.J. is detailed as N.C.O. in charge He will render a Nominal Roll of the men left by Companies to the Adjutant, 2/6th Manch R. at 7 p.m. to-morrow.

7. SANITATION. All hutments and surroundings must be left in a scrupulously clean condition, and fires should be left burning.

8. Completion of relief will be immediately reported by BAB II Code.

9. ACKNOWLEDGE.

Issued at 8.30 PM

(Sgd) John A.Scholfield, Capt.
Adjutant,
2/7th Battalion Manchester Regiment.

Copy No.1. Retained.
2. 2/8th Manch R.
3. C.O.H.Q.Coy.
4. O.C.A.Coy.
5. C.C.B.Coy.
6. O.C.C.Coy.
7. O.C.D.Coy.
8. T.O.
9. Q.M.
10. M.O.
11. R.S.M.
12. War Diary.
13. " "
14. " "
15. Filed.

ROUTE TABLE

RELIEF OF	COY	BY	COY	5/11th DEPART MOLELLES	ROUTE	
RIGHT FIRING LINE	"A" COY. 2/8th	RELIEVED BY	"C" COY 2/4th	I 1-0 PM	[illegible] INGLIS KEEP	– SEVILLE ROW
CENTRE FIRING LINE	"D" " "	– do –	"B" " "	II 1-30 PM	– DO –	RESERVE TR – [illegible]
LEFT FIRING LINE	"C" " "	– do –	"D" " "	III 2-0 PM	– DO –	RESERVE TR – EMERY ALLEY
RIGHT RESERVE TR	"B" " "	– do –	"A" " "	IV 2-30 PM	– DO –	– RESERVE TR

H.Q 1st Party will leave at 12.30 PM

2nd " " " " after last Company

— NO GUIDES REQUIRED —

11/5/17

SECRET. Copy No ....14....

2/7th Battalion Manchester Regiment Order No.18.

11.6.17.

1. RELIEF. The Battalion will relieve the 2/6th Manch R. in the GAUCHE RIGHT Sector to-morrow 12th instant.

2. ROUTE. Relief will be carried out in accordance with attached route table.

3. MARCH DISCIPLINE. Trenches will be used wherever they exist. If road laid down is under shell fire, another road or open fields should be used.

4. USE OF COVER. Officers or N.C.O's in charge of Parties or Platoons will be especially careful to avoid being seen by the enemy. Should hostile aeroplanes appear Parties should leave the road and lie down. It is particularly important that this relief should not be suspected by the enemy.

5. STORES ETC. Officers valises, blankets, packs (with greatcoats inside) will be packed and dumped outside respective Company Headquarters by 7-45 a.m. The Transport Officer will arrange for limbers to call for these at 8-0 a.m. and convey them to the Quarter-Masters Stores.
Officers trench kit, dixies etc. which are not actually carried up will be dumped outside Company Headquarters and a man put in charge. The Transport Officer will arrange for the Company ration limbers to take these things up, on the way to CLARKS KEEP at night.

6. CONVALESCENT HOME. No.275087.Sgt Bond W.J. is detailed as N.C.O. in charge He will render a Nominal Roll of the men left by Companies to the Adjutant, 2/6th Manch R. at 7 p.m. to-morrow.

7. SANITATION. All billets and surroundings must be left in a scrupulously clean condition, and fires should be left burning.

8. Completion of relief will be immediately reported by BAB XI Code.

9. ACKNOWLEDGE.

Issued at ....

(Sgd) John A.Scholfield, Capt.
Adjutant,
2/7th Battalion Manchester Regiment.

Copy No.1. Retained.
2. 2/6th Manch R.
3. O.C. H.Q. Coy.
4. O.C. A. Coy.
5. O.C. B. Coy.
6. O.C. C. Coy.
7. O.C. D. Coy.
8. T.O.
9. Q.M.
10. M.O.
11. R.S.M.
12. War Diary.
13. " "
14. " "
15. Filed.

RELIEF TABLE

RELIEF OF	COY.	BY	AT	[illegible]	[illegible]
[illegible] LINE	"B" [illegible]	[illegible]	"C" [illegible]	I	[illegible]
CENTRE FIRING LINE	"D" " "	— " —	"D" "	II	[illegible]
LEFT FIRING LINE	"C" " "	— " —	"D"	III	[illegible]
[illegible] TR.	"B" " "	— " —	"D" "	IV	[illegible]

H.Q. 1st [illegible]

COY 2nd " [illegible]

— NO GUIDES REQUIRED —

SECRET. Copy No ....13....

2/7th Battalion Manchester Regiment Order No.18.

11.5.17.

1. **RELIEF.** The Battalion will relieve the 2/8th Manch R. in the GAMBRIN RIGHT Sector to-morrow 12th instant.

2. **ROUTE.** Relief will be carried out in accordance with attached route table.

3. **MARCH DISCIPLINE.** Trenches will be used wherever they exist. If road laid down is under shell fire, another road or open fields should be used.

4. **USE OF COVER.** Officers or N.C.O's in charge of Parties or Platoons will be especially careful to avoid being seen by the enemy. Should hostile aeroplanes appear Parties should leave the road and lie down. It is particularly important that this relief should not be suspected by the enemy.

5. **STORES ETC.** Officers valises, blankets, packs (with greatcoats inside) will be packed and dumped outside respective Company Headquarters by 7-45 a.m. The Transport Officer will arrange for limbers to call for these at 8-0 a.m. and convey them to the Quarter-Masters Stores.
Officers trench kit, dixies etc. which are not actually carried up will be dumped outside Company Headquarters and a man put in charge. The Transport Officer will arrange for the Company ration limbers to take these things up, on the way to CLARKS KEEP at night.

6. **CONVALESCENT HOME.** No.275067.Sgt Bond W.J. is detailed as N.C.O. in charge He will render a Nominal Roll of the men left by Companies to the Adjutant, 2/6th Manch R. at 7 p.m. to-morrow.

7. **SANITATION.** All hutments and surroundings must be left in a scrupulously clean condition, and fires should be left burning.

8. Completion of relief will be immediately reported by BAB II Code.

9. ACKNOWLEDGE.

Issued at 8.30 PM

(Sgd) John A.Scholfield, Capt.
Adjutant,
2/7th Battalion Manchester Regiment.

Copy No.1. Retained.
2. 2/8th Manch R.
3. O.C.H.Q.Coy.
4. O.C.A.Coy.
5. O.C.B.Coy.
6. O.C.C.Coy.
7. O.C.D.Coy.
8. T.O.
9. Q.M.
10. M.O.
11. R.S.M.
12. War Diary.
13. " "
14. " "
15. Filed.

ROUTE TABLE

RELIEF OF	COY.	BY	COY.	[illegible]	DEPOT [illegible]	ROUTE
RIGHT FIRING LINE	A coy 7/8	Relieved by	C 9/1	I	1.0 pm	[illegible]
CENTRE FIRING LINE	D " "	" "	B 9/1	II	1.30 pm	[illegible]
LEFT FIRING LINE	C " "	" "	D 9/1	III	2.0 pm	[illegible]
RIGHT RESERVE TR.	B " "	" "	A 9/1	IV	2.30 pm	[illegible] RESERVE TRENCH

H. Q. COY. 1st Party will leave at 12.30 pm
2nd Party will leave after last Company

NO GUIDES REQUIRED

11/5/17

Army Form C. 2118.

2/7 Manchester Regt

Vol 4

WAR DIARY
or
~~INTELLIGENCE SUMMARY~~

(Erase heading not required.)

Instructions regarding War Diaries and Intelligence Summaries are contained in F. S. Regs., Part II. and the Staff Manual respectively. Title Pages will be prepared in manuscript.

Place	Date	Hour	Summary of Events and Information	Remarks and references to Appendices
CAMBRIN RIGHT	1-6-17 to 5-6-17		3 OR wounded 1 OR wounded (S.I.)	
"	4-6-17	12.15PM	Order No 19 issued for relief by 2/8 Bn Manchester Regiment Bn in Reserve in NOYELLES	
NOYELLES	5-6-17		1 OR wounded	
"	10-6-17	3-30PM	Order No 20 issued for relief of 2/8 Bn Man Regt by Bn	
CAMBRIN RT.	12-6-17		1 OR wounded	
"	13-6-17	2 AM	2/Lieut Battersby killed (gas shell) 1 OR killed (gas shell) 12 OR wounded (gassed) 2 OR wounded	
"	14-6-17		1 OR killed	
"	15-6-17		1 OR died of wounds	
"	16-6-17		4 OR wounded	
"	16-6-17	10.45PM	Order No 21 issued for Bn relief by 2/8 Bn Man Regt. 2/7 goes in to Support. ×	
ANNEQUIN	21-6-17		Order No 22 ditto ditto ditto 22nd Bn Royal Fusiliers Battalion marched to BEUVRY thence by bus to Divn Concentration Area. Billets at LAPUGNOY	
LAPUGNOY	24-6-17	8.45PM	Order No 23 issued for move of Bn to PETIT SYNTHE près Dunkirk by train Bn entrained from FOUQUEREUIL	
			× Reinforcements received at ANNEQUIN 97 OR on 20/6/17 54 OR on 21/6/17 & 40 OR on 22/6/17	
PETIT SYNTHE.	26-6-17		Bn in billets at PETIT SYNTHE Training will commence at once	
"	26-6-17		Reinforcements received 68 OR and 62 OR	
"	27-6-17		Strength of the Battalion 44 officers (including MO) and 978 (including 5 RAMC 1 Armourer Sgt)	
	28-6-17 29-6-17 30-6-17		Battalion in training at PETITE SYNTHE	

W Woodward Lt-Col,
Comdng 2/7th Bn. Manch. Regt.

2449 Wt. W14957/M90 750,000 1/16 J.B.C. & A. Forms/C.2118/12.

RELIEF DAY. 5.6.17.

elief of.	Coy.		Coy.		Place.		Time.	Routes
ight Firing Line.	"C" 2/7	by	"A" 2/8	which will pass	INGLIS KEEP	at	8-45 p.m.	GORDON ALLEY, BARTS ALLEY, SAVILLE ROW.
entre Firing ine.	"A" "	"	"C" "	"	"	"	9-15 p.m.	GORDON ALLEY, BARTS ALLEY, LEFT BOYAU.
eft iring ine.	"D" "	"	"B" "	"	CLARKS KEEP	"	8-45 p.m.	QUARRY ALLEY.
ight eserve.	"B" "	"	"D" "	"	INGLIS KEEP	"	9-45 p.m.	GORDON ALLEY, BARTS ALLEY, LEFT BOYAU.

eft eserve. "B" 2/6th " ? 2/5th Relief to be complete by 8-45 p.m.

ailway eserve. "A" 2/6th will move off at 6-0 p.m. After taking over No.1. Coy. CAMERIN LEFT, they will provide Platoon Guides to take the Corps Cavalry to Positions as under:-

1 Officer, 20 O.R. RAILWAY RESERVE TRENCH.

2 Officers.40 O.R. CENTRAL KEEP.

An Officer will be left at Company Headquarters, RAILWAY RESERVE, to hand over stores and documents.

SECRET.   Copy No ..14....

2/7th Battalion Manchester Regiment Order No.20.

10.6.17.

1. RELIEF. The Battalion will relieve the 2/8th Manch R. in the GAMBRIN RIGHT SECTOR to-morrow 11.6.17.

2. ROUTE. Route and Time in accordance with attached Table.

3. EVACUATION OF STORES. The Limbers that bring up Rations to-night will take mens packs and blankets to Stores. They should be stacked outside their respective Company Headquarters.
The Transport Officer will arrange to send to each Company to-morrow morning, one Limber, in time for it to be loaded up.
O's C.Coys. will arrange their own loading and unloading parties.

4. MARCH DISCIPLINE. Trenches will be used wherever they exist. If road laid down is under shell fire, another road or open field should be used.

5. USE OF COVER. Officers or N.C.O's in charge of Parties or Platoons will be especially careful to avoid being seen by the enemy. Should hostile aeroplanes appear, parties should leave the road and lie down. It is particularly important that this relief should not be suspected by the enemy.

6. SANITATION. All Hutments and surroundings should be left in a scrupulously clean condition, and fires left burning.

7. INSPECTION. The Medical Officer will inspect the Company Lines immediately after their departure.

8. Completion of relief will be immediately reported by BAB II Code.

9. ACKNOWLEDGE.

Issued at 3.30 pm

(Sgd) John A.Scholfield, Captain,
Adjutant,
2/7th Battalion Manchester Regiment.

Copy No.1. Retained.
2. 2/8th Manch R.
3. 2/6th " "
4. O.C.A.Coy.
5. O.C.B.Coy.
6. O.C.C.Coy.
7. O.C.D.Coy.
8. O.C.H.Q.Coy.
9. T.O.
10. Q.M.
11. M.O.
12. R.S.M.
13. War Diary.
14. " "
15. " "
16. Filed.

RELIEF DAY. 11.6.17.

Relief of.	Coy.		Coy.		Place.		Time.	Route.
CENTRE FIRING LINE.	"C" 2/8	by	"B" 2/7	which will pass	CLARKES KEEP	at	3-30 am.	QUARRY ALLEY, LEFT BOYAU.
RIGHT FIRING LINE.	"A" 2/8	"	"D" 2/7	"	"	"	3-45 am.	GORDON ALLEY, BARTS ALLEY, SAVILLE ROW.
LEFT FIRING LINE.	"B" 2/8	"	"A" 2/7	"	"	"	4-00 am.	QUARRY ALLEY.
RIGHT RESERVE TRENCH.	"D" 2/8	"	"C" 2/7	"	"	"	4-15 am.	GORDON ALLEY, BARTS ALLEY.

"H.Q" Coy. will leave at 5-0 a.m.

RELIEF TABLE. 17.8.17.

Relief of.	Coy.		Coy.	New Position.	Route.
RIGHT FIRING LINE.	"D" 2/8	will relieve	"D" 2/7	LA TOURBIERE	SAVILLE ROW - RESERVE TRENCH - LEFT BOYAU - QUARRY ALLEY - WINDY CORNER - VILLAGE LINE
CENTRE FIRING LINE.	"C" "	"	"B" "	RESERVE TRENCH (LEFT)	LEFT BOYAU - RESERVE TRENCH.
LEFT FIRING LINE.	"B" "	"	"A" "	RAILWAY RESERVE TRENCH.	QUARRY ALLEY - RAILWAY RESERVE TRENCH.
RIGHT RESERVE TRENCH.	"A" "	"	"C" "	VILLAGE LINE (RIGHT)	BARTS ALLEY - CENTRAL KEEP - CANNON STREET - QUARRY ALLEY.

"H.Q" Coy. will go via CANNON STREET - QUARRY ALLEY - VILLAGE LINE - No.1 TRACK TO ANNEQUIN.

The R.S.M. will detail a N.C.O. i/c Loading Party at CLARKES KEEP.

SECRET. Copy No ..13..

2/7th Battalion Manchester Regiment Order No.21.

16.6.17.

1. RELIEF. The Battalion will be relieved by the 2/8th Manch R. in the CAMBRIN RIGHT SUB-SECTOR, to-morrow 17.6.17. Instructions are that the Battalion Relief will start at 5-0 p.m. and be completed by 10-0 p.m.

2. DISPOSITIONS OF COMPANIES IN SUPPORT.

LA TOURBIERE.	"D" Coy.
VILLAGE LINE (RIGHT)	"C" "
RAILWAY RESERVE TRENCH	"A" "
RESERVE TRENCH (LEFT)	"B" "

O's C.Coys. in Support will take over Standing Orders from the Officer left behind by the Company which he is relieving.

3. TIME AND ROUTE. Time and Route as per attached Table.

4. USE OF COVER. Parties moving in Relief over the open must not be larger than Platoons, and the minimum distance of 300 yards must be kept between Parties.

5. AEROPLANE OBSERVER. Each Platoon Commander will tell off an Aeroplane Observer.

6. HANDING OVER. Receipts will be given for all Maps, Documents and Trench Stores handed over, and copies forwarded to Bn.H.Q. by 9-0 a.m. on 18.6.17.
Emergency Stores will be shewn separately

7. TRANSPORT ARRANGEMENTS. O.C."D" Coy. will make necessary arrangements with the Transport Officer for Officers Valises, and Mens Packs to be taken to LA TOURBIERE, and also for a Limber to take his Lewis Guns, Dixies etc. from CLARKES KEEP. The Transport Officer will arrange for a Limber for "H.Q" and the Mess Cart to be at CLARKES KEEP at 5-0 p.m. on 17.6.17.

8. SIGNALLERS COURSE. The men who were undergoing a Course in Signalling at NOYELLES, will report to the Signalling Officer at Bn. H.Q. at 9-0 a.m. on Monday 18.6.17. These men will be attached to "H.Q" Coy. for Rations and Billets from and including that day, whilst the Battalion is in Support.

9. RUNNERS. Battalion Runners will report to the Quarter-Master at 9-0 a.m. on Monday 18.6.17, and will be attached to him whilst the Battalion is in Support.
O's C.Coys. will detail Runners to report to Bn.H.Q. at 9-0 a.m. and 6-0 p.m. daily.

10. SANITATION. All dug-outs, tunnels and trenches will be left in a scrupulously clean condition.
Petrol Tins will be left filled with water, and fires in Cookhouses burning.

11. Completion of Relief will be immediately reported by BAB II Code.

12. PIONEER PLATOON. The Pioneer Platoon will report to O.C."D" Coy. at 8-0 pm on Sunday 17.6.17, and will be acommodated and rationed by him whilst the Battalion is in Support.

13. A C K N O W L E D G E.

Issued at 10-45 p.m.

(Sgd) John A.Scholfield.
Captain,
Adjt, 2/7th Bn. Manchester Regt.

Copy No.1. Retained. No.2. 2/8th Manch R. 3. to 7. Coys.
8. T.O. 9. Q.M. 10. M.O.
11. R.S.M. 12 to 14. War Diary. 15. Filed.

S E C R E T. Co y No 13.....

2/7th Battalion Manchester Regiment O eration Order No [illegible].

IN THE FIELD. 21.6.17.

REFERENCE BETHUNE COMBINED
SHEET 1/40.000.

O P E R A T I O N S.

1. RELIEF. The Battalion will be relieved in SU ORT AND VILLAGE LINE by the 22nd BATTALION THE ROYAL FUSILIERS to-day 21.6.17.

2. GUIDES. One er Com any will meet relieving Com anies at Battalion Headquarters F.30 a 3/7 at 7-0. .m. to-day. In addition each Com any will detail one Officer to meet relieving Com any at the same lace. This Officer will remain with the relieving Com any until 12-0.noon to-morrow 22.6.17.
He will then re ort to his Com any at LA UGNOY.

3. DOCUMENTS. MA S.ETC. All Defence Schemes, Secret Ma s, Trench Stores, etc will be handed over to relieving Com any and recei ts obtained.
All 1/10.000 - 1/5.000 - 1/40.000 - ma s now in ossession of Com anies will NOT be handed over, but ke t.

4. ROUTE. Com anies will march inde endently to LA UGNOY when relieved via BEUVRY and BETHUNE.

5. FORMATIONS. By sections to ANNEQUIN. By latoons to BEUVRY.

6. INTERVALS. 200 yards between latoons. 100 yards between sections.

7. TRAFFIC CONTROL. The rovost Sergeant will arrange to control all traffic from RAILWAY HOUSE (G.[illegible] b [illegible]) and entrance to [illegible] ALLEY back to F 30 b 1/6.

8. COM LETION OF RELIEF. Com letion of relief will be re orted immediately by B.A.B.II Code.

A D M I N I S T R A T I O N.

1. TRANS ORT. Two A.S.C.Wagons have alre dy been allotted to the Trans ort for the move.
The Trans ort Officer will arrange for two Limbers to be at the resent Battalion Headquarters at 10-0. m to-night. Com anies will arrange to carry their Lewis Guns etc. to this oint.
Yukon acks and Cords,im rovised with girth and surcingles, also gun ammunition carriers will NOT be handed over, but taken away.
He will arrange trans ort of stores etc to LA UGNOY with the Quarter-Master.

2. BILLETS. (a) All concerned are res onsible that all Billets, trenches, Trans ort Lines, Store Rooms etc are left absolutely clean.
The [illegible] Section will be attached to "D" ortion of H.Q.Com any until further notice as a ermanent fatigue.
(b) The Battalion will roceed into billets at LA UGNOY.
2nd.Lt.Rudd will roceed to LA UGNOY this morning with the C.Q.M.S's and arrange billets. He will re ort to the MAIRE for billeting lists.
(c) He will arrange for the C.Q.M.S's to await their Com anies at the Traffic Control ost on the BETHUNE

/ROAD

SECRET. Copy No. 17.

1/7th Battalion Manchester Regiment Operation Order No.2[illegible].

IN THE FIELD, [illegible].17.

1\. MOVE. The Battalion will move by Rail in accordance with attached Programme.
The special attention of all concerned is drawn to the Notes.

2\. DRESS. [illegible] Steel Helmets will be carried on the left shoulder.

3\. DISCIPLINE. The strictest discipline will be maintained during the train journey, and all instructions laid down in this Office No. [illegible] of [illegible].17, will be carefully carried out by O's C. Coys.

4\. LOADING PARTIES. O's C. "A" and "B" Coys. will each detail Loading Parties of 1 Officer and 20 Other Ranks to report to Lieut. BROWN at the Entraining Station at [illegible] a.m.
These parties will report to the [illegible] immediately on arrival at the Entraining Station.

5\. SURPLUS STORES. The Quarter-master will arrange with the Transport Officer and [illegible] to dump all surplus Stores at the Station.
The [illegible] will arrange a suitable place with the Brigade [illegible] (Capt. [illegible] Maxwell, [illegible] Bn. Manch R.)

6\. OFFICERS BAGGAGE. Officers Baggage will be stacked outside the respective Messes not later than [illegible] p.m. on [illegible].
The Transport Officer will arrange collection.

7\. BILLETS. O's C. Coys. will carry out a final inspection of Billets before departure, and will render a certificate to this Office that all Billets have been left clean and in good order, and that there are no outstanding claims for damages.

8\. SANITATION. All temporary Latrines will be filled in.
The Medical Officer will carry out a final inspection after the departure of the Troops, and will render a certificate that all Latrines have been filled in, and left in good order.

9\. A C K N O W L E D G E.

(Sgd) John A. Scholfield, Captain,
Adjutant,
1/7th Battalion Manchester Regiment.

Issued at [illegible] p.m.

Copy No.1. Retained.
2\. O.C.A.Coy.
3\. O.C.B.Coy.
4\. O.C.C.Coy.
5\. O.C.D.Coy.
6\. O.C.H.Q.Coy.
7\. T.O.
8\. Q.M.
9\. M.O.
10\. O.i/c Loading Party.
11\. R.S.M.
12\. War Diary.
13\. " "
14\. " "
15\. [illegible] Bde.

SHEET No.2. ADMINISTRATION. (Cont'd)

2. BILLETS. (Cont'd) Road E 19 c 70.05 at the following times :-
H.Q.Company .... [illegible]
A.B.C. & D Coys ...... 10-0.a.m.

3. DRAFT. The draft of [illegible] other ranks which arrived last night will be rationed and accommodated by H.Q. Company until further orders.

4. COMPANY STRENGTH. All ranks attached to the 170th Tunnelling Company R.E. will rejoin their Companies in time for them to move with their respective Companies to-night.

5. SUPPLIES. On receiving orders to entrain the Quarter-Master will carry the number of days' reserved rations that are sufficient for the journey by train. Supply Wagons will be loaded with another day's rations.

6. BLANKETS ETC. All Blankets in possession will be handed over to the incoming Unit at Quarter-Master's Stores, together with any other stores that are unable to be carried owing to lack of Transport.

7. A C K N O W L E D G E.

[illegible]
Captain.
Adjutant. 1/7th Battalion Manchester Regt.

Issued at 6-0 am

Copy No 1 Retained.
" " 2 127th Brigade.
" " 3 O.C. [illegible] Bn.Royal Fusiliers.
" " 4 O.C. "A" Co.
" " 5 O.C. "B" "
" " 6 O.C. "C" "
" " 7 O.C. "D" "
" " 8 O.C. "H.Q." Co.
" " 9 Medical Officer.
" " 10 Quarter-Master.
" " 11 Transport Officer.
" " 12 R.S.M.
" " 13 War Diary.
" " 14 " "
" " 15 " "
" " 16 Filed.

SECRET.

2/7th Battalion Manchester Regiment.

PROGRAMME FOR ENTRAINMENT.

	Detail.	Entrain.	Train No.	Date.	Depart.	Detrain.
1.	Battalion <u>less</u> "D" Co. Cooker and Team.		20.	26.8.17.	5-25 a.m.	LOON PLAGE.
2.	"D" Coy. Cooker and Team.		22.	26.8.17.	[illegible]-25 a.m.	LOON PLAGE.

N.B.1. Lieut. J. Brown is detailed as R.R.T.O. and will supervise entraining and detraining of all Troops and Transport, on Train No.20.
Captain R.L.Bolton will detail an Officer to supervise entraining and detraining on Train No.22.

2. The Transport Officer will arrange for all Transport to be at the Station precisely three hours before the time of departure.

3. O's C.Coys. will arrange to arrive at the Station one and a quarter hours before time of departure.
Order of assembly at Station for Train No.20 "B" "C" "A" "H.Q".

4. Rations for 26th inst, will be carried on man.
Rations for 27th inst, will be carried on Supply Wagons with Battalion.
Rations for 28th inst, will be carried on D.S.C.

Page I

Instructions regarding War Diaries and Intelligence Summaries are contained in F. S. Regs., Part II. and the Staff Manual respectively. Title Pages will be prepared in manuscript.

WAR DIARY
or
~~INTELLIGENCE SUMMARY~~
(Erase heading not required.)

Army Form C. 2118.

Place	Date	Hour	Summary of Events and Information	Remarks and references to Appendices
PETITE SYNTHE	1.7.17		Battalion in training at PETITE SYNTHE	AS
	2.7.17		17 Reinforcements received (O.R.)	AS
	3.7.17		Reinforcements received (3 O.R.)	AS
	4.7.17 – 7.7.17		Battalion in training at PETITE SYNTHE	AS
	8.7.17		Operation order No 24 issued for move of battalion into billets at TETEGHEM.	
TETEGHEM	9.7.17		Battalion marched to TETEGHEM	
	10.7.17		Received copy Preliminary order for move to COXYDE. Order "Prepare to move at one hours notice" recd 11. 0 p.m.	AS
	11.7.17		Operation order No 35 recd for move of battalion into ~~billets~~ at ~~GHYVELDE~~. COXYDE BAINS. This order	AS
	~~12.7.17~~		cancelled & fresh orders recd for move to GHYVELDE.	AS
			Operation order No 25 issued for move of battalion to GHYVELDE	AS
GHYVELDE	12.7.17		Battalion marched to GHYVELDE (huts).	AS
	13.7.17		Battalion in training at GHYVELDE	AS
	14.7.17		Preliminary order received for move to COXYDE BAINS. Operation order No 26 for move of battalion to COXYDE BAINS issued.	AS
COXYDE BAINS	15.7.17		Battalion moved to COXYDE BAINS and took over Coast Defence from 2nd WELSH REGT.	AS
	16.7.17		Battalion held LEFT Sub-sector of coast defence line.	AS
	21.7.17		Operation order No 27 issued for relief of Bn. by 2/8th Bn. Manchester Regt.	AS
CAMP LEFEVRE	22.7.17		Bn was relieved by 2/8th Bn. Mchr. Regt, and moved to CAMP LEFEVRE near OOST DUNKERKE BAINS	AS
	24.7.17	4-30 PM	Operation order No 29 issued Bn to relieve 1/4 KOYLI in NIEUPORT RESERVE night of 24.7.17	JHS
			Bn held up during relief owing to severe bombardment	
	25.7.17		In Bivouac Relief completed early hours of 26/7/17	JHS
NIEUPORT	26.7.17		Heavily shelled throughout the day	JHS
	27.7.17		ditto ditto ditto	JHS
			Bn bivouac with exception of garrisons each night from 25/7/17	
	28.7.17		Shelled in bivouac by German gas shells (mustard) only a few casualties	JHS

2449 Wt. W14957/M90 750,000 1/16 J.B.C. & A. Forms/C.2118/12.

Page II

Instructions regarding War Diaries and Intelligence Summaries are contained in F. S. Regs., Part II. and the Staff Manual respectively. Title Pages will be prepared in manuscript.

WAR DIARY
or
INTELLIGENCE SUMMARY
(Erase heading not required.)

Army Form C. 2118.

Place	Date	Hour	Summary of Events and Information	Remarks and references to Appendices
NIEUPORT	30/7/17	5-15 PM 7-10 PM	Bn HQ heavily shelled by 5/9s	JHB
		8 PM	Order No 29 issued Bn to relieve 1/7th West Riding Regt in ~~NIEUPORT~~ LOMBARTZYDE left SUB-SECTOR tonight	JHB
LEFT SUBSECTOR LOMBARTZYDE	31/7/17	6 AM	Relief completed with 1 casualty (1 OR wounded)	JHB
			Casualties for month.	JHB
			16/7/17 1 OR wounded (S1) revolver	
			20/7/17 1 " " accidental	
			22/7/17 1 " "	
			~~22/7/17 3 killed (OR) and 6 OR wounded~~	
			23/7/17 6 OR killed 3 OR killed (gas) 4 OR wounded 14 OR wounded (gas) 1 OR missing	
			25/7/17 3 OR wounded 2nd Lieut Holland wounded (gas) returned to Duty 28/7/17	
			26/7/17 1 OR ~~wounded~~ killed 1 OR Missing	JHB
			27/7/17 1 OR killed	
			28/7/17 2 OR wounded (gas)	
			29/7/17 1 OR killed 2 OR wounded 6 OR wounded (gas)	
			31/7/17 1 OR wounded	
			Total for month Killed 12 Wounded 35 (including 1 S1, 1 acc) Missing 2 Total 49	

[signature] Lieut-Col
Commanding 2/7 Bn Man Regt

2449 Wt. W14957/M90 750,000 1/16 J.B.C. & A. Forms/C.2118/12.

SECRET. Copy No. 13

2/7th Battalion Manchester Regiment Operation Order No.[illegible].

In the Field. [illegible].

1. MOVE. The Battalion will move into Billets at [illegible] to-morrow.

2. ROUTE. [illegible] - CAPELLE - [illegible] to Destination.

3. STARTING POINT. Battalion Starting Point will be at G 18 d [illegible]. Companies and Transport will assemble at Starting Point at [illegible] a.m.

4. ORDER OF MARCH. "B" "C" "H.Q" "D" "A" Coys, Transport.

5. MARCH DISCIPLINE. After leaving Starting Point a minimum distance of 200 yards between Companies will be maintained. Particular attention must be paid to March Discipline, also to the way that all Vehicles and Transport are turned out.

6. DRESS. F.S.M.O. Steel Helmets will be worn.

7. REAR PARTY. O.C."A" Coy. will provide 1 Platoon as Rear Party.

8. HALTS. 5 minutes halt at [illegible] a.m. - after that from 10 minutes before each hour, to the hour.

9. OFFICERS BAGGAGE. Officers Valises and Company Stores will be packed on Transport at [illegible] a.m. Companies will provide small Loading Parties.

10. BILLETS. O's C.Coys. will carry out a final inspection of Billets before departure, and will render a certificate to this Office that all Billets have been left clean and in good order, and that there are no outstanding claims for damages.

11. SANITATION. All temporary Latrines will be filled in. The Medical Officer will carry out a final inspection, and will render a certificate that all latrines have been filled in, and left in good order.

12. LOCATION. O's C.Coys. will send in position of Company Headquarters immediately on arrival at Billets.

13. ACKNOWLEDGE.

(Sgd) Arthur [illegible].
Lieut. & A/Adjt.
2/7th Bn. Manchester Regiment.

Issued at 2-0 pm

Copy No.1. Retained.
2. [illegible]th Bde.
3. O.C."A" Coy.
4. O.C."B" Coy.
5. O.C."C" Coy.
6. O.C."D" Coy.
7. O.C."H.Q" Coy.
8. T.O.
9. Q.M.
10. M.O.
11. R.S.M.
12. War Diary.
13. " "
14. " "
15. Filed.

S E C R E T.   Copy No ......

2/7th Battalion Manchester Regiment Operation Order No.26.

Ref.DUNKERQUE SHEET 12.
1/40,000.

In the Field. 11.7.17.

1. MOVE. The Battalion will move tomorrow to GHYVELDE.

2. ROUTE. Forked roads C 26 c 6.6 - main FURNES road to PONT DE GHYVELDE - GHYVELDE.

3. STARTING POINT. Road Junction I 9 c 5.5 - ½ mile N.W. H.Q.Mess. Companies will assemble at the Starting Point at 5-40.am.

4. ORDER OF MARCH. Band, "A", "H.Q." "B", "C", "D". O.C. "D" Coy. will detail one platoon as Rear Party.

5. DRESS. F.S.M.O. Steel Helmets will be worn.

6. TRANSPORT. All Possible Transport will be packed tonight.Remainder of Company Stores and Officers valises will be at Cross Roads at Church, opposite "B" Coy H.Q. ready for loading at 4-30.am.
Officers Kits will be reduced to a maximum of 35.lbs and all possible mess and orderly room stores reduced to a minimum.
The Quarter-Master will arrange to form a dump at the Q.M. Stores of surplus Officers' Kit and other stores which cannot be carried on transport tomorrow. The surplus kit will be collected tonight and dumped at the Q.M.Stores. The Transport Officer will arrange to have a wagon at each Company H.Q. and Bn.H.Q. at 8-30.pm tonight.

7. BILLETS. O's.C.Coys will carry out a final inspection of billets before departure and will render a certificate to this Office that all billets have been left clean and in good order, and that there are no outstanding claims for damages.

8. SANITATION. All temporary latrines will be filled in. The Medical Officer will carry out a final inspection, and will render a certificate that all latrines have been filled in and left in good order.

9. MARCH DISCIPLINE. After leaving starting point, a minimum distance of 200 yards between Companies will be maintained. Particular attention must be paid to march discipline, also to the way that all vehicles and transport are turned out.

10. BILLETING. Company Billeting N.C.Os. will report to Lt.Morris at Bn.H.Q. at 4-0.am. tomorrow.

11. LOCATION. O's.C.Coys will send in position of Coy.H.Q. immediately on arrival at billets.

12. A C K N O W L E D G E.

(Sgd) Artgur Smithies,
Lieut.& Asst.Adjt.
2/7th Battn.Manchester Regiment.

Issued at 11-30.pm.

Copy No.1. retained. Copy No.3 199th Bde.
" " 2. "A" Co. " " 4 "B" Co.
" " 5. "C" " " " 6 "D" "
" " 7. "H.Q." " " 8 T.O.
" " 9. Q.M. " " 10.M.O.
" " 11, R.S.M. " " 12,War Diary.
" " 13 " "
" " 14 " "
" " 15 Filed.

SECRET. Copy No. ..13...

2/7th Battalion Manchester Regiment Operation Order No. 35.

In the Field. 14.7.17.

1. MOVE. The Battalion will move to-morrow to C[illegible] BAINS.

2. ROUTE. PONT DE [illegible] to Destination.

3. STARTING POINT. PONT DE [illegible].
Companies will assemble at the Starting Point at 8-45 a.m.

4. ORDER OF MARCH. Band, "B" "A" "H.Q" "C" "D".
O.C. "D" Coy. will detail 1 Platoon as Rear Party.

5. DRESS. F.S.M.O. Steel Helmets will be worn.

6. BAGGAGE ETC. All possible Transport will be packed to-night, and Lewis Gun Magazines filled. All Officers Valises and Baggage will as far as possible be loaded to-night.
All Baggage that does not travel on the Limbers or Cookers will be stacked at Bn.H.Q. (Billet No.[illegible], in the Village) by 6-0 a.m. certain to-morrow.
Each Company will provide a Section as Loading Party for loading these.
A Lorry will be available at 8-30 a.m. to-morrow, which will convey Stores etc. to destination.
The R.S.M. will detail a Guard of 1 N.C.O. and 3 men over the dump to-night.
The Quarter-master will provide a Loading Party from "H.Q" (B) Coy. at 6-0 a.m. to-morrow. This party will relieve the Guard which mounts to-night.

7. BILLETS. O's C.Coys. will carry out a final inspection of Billets before departure, and will render a certificate to this Office that all Billets have been left clean, and in good order.

8. SANITATION. All temporary Latrines will be filled in. The Medical Officer will carry out a final inspection, and will render a certificate that all Latrines have been filled in, and left in good order.

9. MARCH DISCIPLINE. After leaving the Starting Point a minimum distance of 200 yards between Companies will be maintained. Particular attention must be paid to March Discipline.

10. LOCATION. O's C.Coys. will send in position of Coy.H.Q. immediately on arrival at destination.

11. ACKNOWLEDGE.

Issued at ....

(Sgd) Arthur Smithies,
Lieut. & A/Adjt.
2/7th Bn. Manchester Regiment.

Copy No. 1. Retained.
2. 199th Inf.Bde.
3. O.C.A.Coy.
4. O.C.B.Coy.
5. O.C.C.Coy.
6. O.C.D.Coy.
7. O.C.H.Q.Coy.
8. T.O.
9. Q.M.
10. M.O.
11. R.S.M.
12. War Diary.
13. " "
14. " "
15. Filed.

SECRET. Copy No ..13....

2/7th Battalion Manchester Regiment Order No.37.

In the Field. 20.7.17.

1. RELIEF. The Battalion will be relieved to-morrow by the 2/8th Bn. Manch R.

2. GUIDES. Companies will send one Guide to be at Cross Roads W.6.a.9.6 at 9-45 a.m.

3. RELIEF OF COMPANIES. Companies of 2/8th Bn. Manch R. will relieve as follows arriving about 10-0 a.m.

"C"	2/8th	relieves	"D"	2/7th.
"A"	"	"	"C"	"
"D"	"	"	"B"	"
"B"	"	"	"A"	"

4. HANDING OVER. Incoming Companies will take over Billets, Trench Stores, Maps, S.A.A. and Grenades, from the Companies relieved. Receipts will be given for all Stores taken over, and copies sent to Bn.H.Q. by 9-0 p.m. to-morrow.

5. ROUTE. On completion of Relief Companies will march independently to CAMP RINCK R.32.d. and take over quarters vacated by 2/8th Bn. Manch R. who will leave one representative per Company to hand over.

6. STORES, ETC. The Transport Officer will have teams for Water Carts and Cookers at the Coy.H.Q. at 8-30 a.m. and a Limber at "B" Coy.H.Q. at same hour.
All other Company Stores and Lewis Guns will be at the Transport Lines at 9-0 a.m. "A" "C" & "D" Coys. will provide Section loading parties at that hour.
The Transport Officer will arrange to move Q.M.Stores, Ammunition etc. to CAMP RINCK in the course of the day.

7. SANITATION. All Billets, Cookhouses etc. will be left scrupulously clean.

8. Completion of Relief will be immediately reported to Bn.H.Q. also completion of Move.
Location of Coy.H.Q. to be immediately sent to Bn.H.Q. on arrival at CAMP RINCK

9. ACKNOWLEDGE.

(Sgd) Arthur Smithies.
Lieut. & A/Adjt.
2/7th Bn. Manchester Regiment.

Issued at ...4 pm....

Copy No.1. Retained.
2. 2/8th Manch R.
3. O.C.H.Q.Coy.
4. O.C.A.Coy.
5. O.C.B.Coy.
6. O.C.C.Coy.
7. O.C.D.Coy.
8. T.O.
9. Q.M.
10. M.O.
11. R.S.M.
12. War Diary.
13. " "
14. " "
15. Filed.

SECRET. Copy No ...13....

ADDENDUM TO

2/7th Battalion Manchester Regiment Order No.27.

In the Field. 20.7.17.

1. **PARA.2.** For CAMP WINCK, R.32.d. Read CAMP LEFEVRE About R.32.c. Delete remainder of para.

2. In each case for CAMP WINCK substitute CAMP LEFEVRE.

3. ACKNOWLEDGE.

(Sgd) Arthur Smithies,
Lieut. & A/Adjt.
2/7th Bn. Manchester Regiment.

Issued at .... 6-45 pm.

Copy No.1. Retained.
2. 2/6th Manch R.
3. O.C.H.Q.Coy.
4. O.C.A.Coy.
5 .O.C.B.Coy.
6. O.C.C.Coy.
7. O.C.D.Coy.
8. T.O.
9. Q.M.
10. M.O.
11. R.S.M.
12. War Diary.
13. " "
14. " "
15. Filed.

SECRET.   Copy No ..13....

2/7th Battalion Manchester Regiment Order No.28.

In the Field, 24.7.17.

1. RELIEF. The Battalion will relieve the 4th K.O.Y.L.I. in the NIEUPORT Reserve Line to-night.
Companies will relieve their opposite Numbers.

2. GUIDES. Guides of the 4th K.O.Y.L.I. will meet the Battalion at TRANSPORT CORNER, H.32.c.30.10 at 11 p.m.

3. MARCHING OUT. Companies will leave Camp in the following order:-
"A" "B" "C" "D" "H.Q". "A" Coy. leaving at 8-30 p.m.
A distance of 200 yards will be maintained between platoons.
E-ach Company Limber will march behind leading platoon of its Company.

4. DRESS. Fighting Order. Water Bottles filled. Rations for the 25th inst. will be carried on the man.

5. STORES ETC. The Company Limbers containing Lewis Guns, Lewis Gun Drums, 4 Camp Kettles, 16 empty petrol tins, and Officers Trench Kits, will be off-loaded at TRANSPORT CORNER, and everything will be carried from thereby hand.

6. ROUTE. OOST DUNKERQUE BAINS - OOST DUNKERQUE - H.31.c.20.35. - ZOUAVE ROAD - NIEUPORT.

7. MARCH DISCIPLINE. March Discipline will be strictly observed. Special attention being paid to keeping touch by connecting files.
Gas Appliances will be worn in the "ALERT" position.

8. HANDING OVER. Receipts will be given for all Trench Stores, Defence Schemes, Maps, Programme of Work begun and proposed, handed over.

9. SANITATION. All Hutments, Latrines, Cookhouses, etc. will be left scrupulously clean.

10. RUNNERS. On arrival at NIEUPORT O's C.Coys. will send two runners to Bn.H.Q. O.C."H.Q" Coy. will arrange for two runners to report to Brigade H.Q.

11. Completion of Relief will be immediately reported to Bn.H.Q. by runner.

12. ACKNOWLEDGE.

(Sgd) John A.Scholfield, Captain,
Adjutant,
2/7th Bn. Manchester Regiment.

Issued at 4-30 p.m.

Copy No.1. Retained.
2. 199th Inf.Bde.
3. O.C.H.Q.Coy.
4. O.C.A.Coy.
5. O.C.B.Coy.
6. O.C.C.Coy.
7. O.C.D.Coy.
8. T.O.
9. Q.M.
10. M.O.
111. R.S.M.
12. War Diary.
13. " "
14. " "
15. Filed.

Confidential

Original

War Diary

of

7/4 Bn The Manchester Regt

from 1.8.17 to 31.8.17

Volume VI

CONFIDENTIAL

WAR DIARY

OF

2/7th Battn. THE MANCHESTER Regt.

FROM:- ~~August~~ July 1st 1917 TO:- ~~August~~ July 31st 1917.

VOLUME No. 5

AKW
2-8-17

Vol 5

Instructions regarding War Diaries and Intelligence Summaries are contained in F. S. Regs., Part II. and the Staff Manual respectively. Title Pages will be prepared in manuscript.

WAR DIARY
or
INTELLIGENCE SUMMARY
(Erase heading not required.)

Army Form C. 2118.

Place	Date	Hour	Summary of Events and Information	Remarks and references to Appendices
LOMBARTZYDE (left) SUB SECTOR	1/8/17		Battalion holding line in LOMBARTZYDE (LEFT) SUBSECTOR. Casualties 3 killed; 7 wounded (one S.I.)	AS
	2/8/17	9.0 a.m.	Raided enemy post at M22 b 80 20 to M22 b 65 30. Casualties this day 1 off. killed; 1 off. wounded; 8 O.R. killed	
	2/8/17		For gallantry this day No 275558 CORPL. LEIGH E was awarded MILITARY MEDAL (19.8.17) 24 O.R. wounded; 6 O.R. missing	AS
	3/8/17		Operation order No 30 issued. Casualties 4 O.R. killed; 15 O.R. wounded.	AS
ST. IDESBALD	4/8/17		Battalion under canvas at ST. IDESBALD training.	AS
	9/8/17		Operation order No 31 issued.	AS
OOST DUNKERKE BAINS	10/8/17		Battalion took over YORKSHIRE CAMP, OOST DUNKERKE BAINS.	AS
	11/8/17		Order No 32 issued	AS
NIEUPORT BAINS (Right) SUB SECTOR	12/8/17		Battalion took over the line in NIEUPORT BAINS (RIGHT) SUBSECTOR. Casualties 1 off. 3 O.R. wounded	AS
	17/8/17		Ration party shelled on way up to line. Casualties 3 killed 14 wounded (one S.I.)	AS
	20/8/17		Order No 35 issued.	AS
COXYDE BAINS	22/8/17		Battalion relieved and went into billets at COXYDE BAINS. Casualties 1 off wounded (Gas) 1 O.R. wounded (Gas)	AS
	25/8/17		Working party carrying shell to NIEUPORT BAINS suffered casualties 10 O.R. wounded (gas)	AS
	26/8/17		Order No 36 issued.	AS
LA PANNE	27/8/17		Battalion relieved 1/7th Bn. WEST RIDING REGIMENT in coast defence LA PANNE (left sector)	AS
	29/8/17		1 O.R. wounded (accidental).	AS
	31/8/17		Strength of battalion including attached 40 officers 825 O. Ranks.	AS

[signature] Lt Col.
Comdg. 2/7th Bn Manchester Regt

SECRET. Copy No ....

2/7th Battalion Manchester Regiment Order No.50.

Reference 1.20000, COXYDE and LOMBARTZYDE SHEETS.

In the Field, 3.8.17.

1. RELIEF. The Battalion will be relieved in the LOMBARTZYDE SECTOR, on the night of August 3/4th by the 1/5th West Riding Regt.

2. INSTRUCTIONS. Instructions regarding crossing of bridges and bridges allotted are attached marked "B".

3. ROUTE. The Battalion will move out in the following order:- "H.Q.","A","B","D", "C" via PUTNEY BRIDGE - The most westerly road of the Town - Pt M.34.a.60.40 - OOST DUNKERKE ROAD - COXYDE- COXYDE BAINS - ST. IDESBALDE.

4. TRANSPORT. The Transport Officer will arrange for 5 Limbers to report at the present ration dump, M.34.a.7.2. at 11-30 p.m.
The R.S.M. will detail a guide to direct these Limbers to the junction of the most westerly NIEUPORT ROAD and OOST DUNKERKE ROAD facing SOUTH.
Lewis Guns will be loaded here. The Officer of the leading platoon of each Company will detail a reliable N.C.O to remain with the Company Limber until all four Lewis Guns, etc of his Company have been loaded. This N.C.O. will accompany the Limber in rear of the last Platoon of his Company.

5. MOVEMENT. Outgoing Companies will not march with less than 200 yards between platoons, but the Platoons on relief will march straight out of the town along the routes without waiting to see that the platoon next behind is at this distance.
The Battalion will move by Companies to ST IDESBALDE after Pt.M.36.c.60.85., is reached.

6. GUIDES.
(a) 1 Officer per Company and 1 Guide per Platoon will meet 1/5th West Riding Regt. at Road Junction M.33.b.80.40 at 9-30 p.m.
They will report to Bn.H.Q. on their way down.
(b) Company Guides will meet their Companies at X.13.b.50.35. (junction of roads in COXYDE) and lead to billets.
(c) The Transport Officer has arranged for Officers Chargers to wait at the Western End of OOST DUNKERKE until picked up by their owners.

7. HANDING OVER. On relief the following will be handed over :-
(a) All trench stores.
(b) Defence Schemes.
(c) All ordinary trench maps with the exception of Sheets 12 S.W. 1,2,3 and 4 Scale 1.10000, and 3 S.W. 1.20000.
Secret Trench Maps will be retained with the exception of those giving special information added since issue.
All other maps will be retained.
All photographs will be handed over.
Receipts will be obtained for all Trench Stores etc. handed over, and duplicate copies forwarded to this Office, on completion of relief.
(d) Details of work in progress. Condition of tracks etc.
(e) All details of patrol reports and information as regards NO MANS LAND should be handed over and sketches of NO MANS LAND containing all possible information should be prepared.

8. COMPLETION OF RELIEF. Completion of Company Reliefs will be reported to Bn.H.Q by an Officer as his last Platoon reaches PUTNEY BRIDGE on the way out.
Report will be in writing. Cod word "CRUST" will be used.

9. ACKNOWLEDGE

(sgd) JOHN A SCHOLFIELD.
Capt. Adjutant.
2/7th Bn. Manchester Regiment.

Issued at...2.45 p.m.

Distribution over

Copy No. 1. Retained.
" " 2. 199th Inf.Bde.
" " 3. 1/5th West Riding Regt.
" " 4. 2nd in command.
" " 5. 1/7th West Riding Regt.
" " 6. O.C.A.Company.
" " 7. O.C.B.Company.
" " 8. O.C.C.Company.
" " 9. O.C.D.Company.
" " 10. O.C.H.Q.Company
" " 11. T.O.
" " 12. Q.M.
" " 13. M.O.
" " 14. R.S.M.
" " 15. War Diary.
" " 16. " "
" " 17. " "
" " 18. Filed.

SECRET. Copy No ...14...

2/7th Battalion Manchester Regiment Order No.51.

Reference Map,
Sheet 11 S.E. 1.20,000. In the Field. 9.8.17.

1. MOVE. The Battalion will exchange Camps with the 2/10th Bn. Manch R. to-morrow, taking over YORKSHIRE (JUNIAC) CAMP, about R.3.c. (Central).

2. ROUTE. COXYDE BAINS - ~~MIDDLESEX (RINCK)~~ CAMP - YORKSHIRE (JUNIAC) CAMP.

3. ORDER AND TIME OF MARCH. "A" Coy. 9-30 a.m. "B" Coy. 9-45 a.m. "C" Coy. 10-0 a.m. "D" 10-15 a.m. "H.Q" 10-30 a.m.
Movement will be by Companies as far as COXYDE BAINS, and then by Platoons to the Camp.
Interval of 200 yards between platoons.

4. TRANSPORT. Transport Officer will arrange for Company L.G.Limbers, 1 H.Q. Coy. Limber, and 1 Limber for Officers Baggage to report at 8-30 a.m. Limbers will be packed on the road.
The above vehicles will be taken together with Mess Cart, Maltese Cart, Water Carts, and Field Kitchens by the Transport Officer to the new Camp at 9-30 a.m. via COXYDE and OOST DUNKERKE.
C.Q.M.S's will proceed to the Camp ahead of their Companies, ~~xxx~~ to take over Huts etc.

5. RELIEF DAY. The Battalion will relieve the 2/8th Bn. Manch R. in the Right Sub-Sector, Front Line, on the night August 11/12th.
O's C.Coys. will arrange for 1 Officer per Company to report to Major John E.Rowbotham at 8-30 a.m. on 10.8.17.
Rations should be carried for the day as they will make a reconnaissance of the above Sector.
Further orders will be issued later as regards this relief.
Q.M.Stores and Transport Lines will remain where they are for the present.

6. ACKNOWLEDGE.

Issued at ...7.15 pm...

(Sgd) John A.Scholfield. Captain, Adjutant,
2/7th Bn. Manchester Regiment.

Copy No.1. Retained.
2. 199th Inf.Bde.
3. 2/10th Manch R.
4. 2nd in Command.
5 to 9. Coys.
10. T.O.
11. Q.M.
12. M.O.
13. R.S.M.
14 to 16. War Diary.
17. Filed.

SECRET. Copy No 14

2/7th Battalion Manchester Regiment Order No.32.

Reference Map, In the Field, 11.8.17.
Sheet 12 S.W.1. 1.10000.

1. RELIEF. The Battalion will relieve the 2/8th Bn. Manch R. on the night of 11/12th August 1917, in the Right Sub-Sector, NIEUPORT BAINS SECTOR.

2. DISTRIBUTION. Companies will be distributed as follows:-
"A" Coy .... LEFT FIRING LINE.
"B" " .... RIGHT FIRING LINE.
"C" " ..... RIGHT SUPPORT.
"D" " .... RESERVE.

3. GUIDES AND MOVEMENT. Platoon Guides will meet relieving Platoons at M.26.d.0.4. at 9-30 p.m.
Companies will move off in the following order:-
"B" "A" "C" "H.Q" "D"
First Company moving off at 8-30 p.m.
Movement to be by Platoons at 200 yards interval.

4. TRANSPORT. Lewis Gun Limbers will move at the rear of the leading Platoon of each Company.
The Transport Officer will detail a Limber in addition, for "H.Q" Coy.
Each Company will take 5 empty petrol tins in its Limber.

5. DETAILS. Companies will only take 1 cook into the Line with them. The rest together with surplus "H.Q" Coy. will be billeted at the Q.M.Stores, and will be under Lieut.F.M.pott for discipline. This Officer will detail a carrying party of 15 Other Ranks nightly from the personnel behind the Line, for carrying "D" Coys. Rations.

6. RATIONS. Ration arrangements in accordance with attached.
Rations for to-morrow will be carried on the man, and will be distributed before the Battalion moves off.

7. GAS GUARD. "C" and "D" Coys. will detail a Gas Guard for "H.Q" alternately, commencing with "C" Coy. to-night.
The Guard will report to the R.S.M. on Completion of Relief.

8. TRENCH STORES ETC. Copies of receipts given will be forwarded to Bn.H.Q. by 9 a.m. on 12.8.17.

9. Completion of Relief will be reported by Code word "COPPER"

10. ACKNOWLEDGE.

(Sgd) John A.Scholfield,
Capt. & Adjt.
2/7th Bn. Manchester Regiment.

Issued at 3 p.m.

Copy No.1. Retained.
2. 199th Inf.Bde.
3. 2/8th Manch R.
4. 2nd in Command.
5. O.C.A.Coy.
6. O.C.B.Coy.
7. O.C.C.Coy.
8. O.C.D.Coy.
9. O.C.H.Q.Coy.
10. T.O.
11. Q.M.
12. M.O.
13. R.S.M.
14. War Diary.
15. " "
16. " "
17. Filed.

8/7th Battalion Manchester Regiment.

Battalion in Right Sub-Sector (Dune).

"A" STANDING ORDERS.

1. The Regimental Transport will convey Rations each night to Ration Dump at M.28.d.0.4.
Time of arrival, approximately 10 p.m.

2. O.C. Reserve Company will provide carrying parties (18 O.R) for each Company in Front Line and Support(3 Coys.).
O's C. Front Line and Support Companies will each detail an Officer to report to Reserve Company H.Q. at 9 p.m. nightly to take charge of their carrying parties and proceed to Ration Dump.
O.C. Details will provide carrying party (18 O.R) for Reserve Coy.
O.C. Reserve Company will detail an Officer to take charge of this party.
O.C.H.Q.Coy. will arrange carrying party for H.Q. Mess and H.Q.Coy.

3. Carrying parties will deliver Rations to Company H.Q. and return.

4. Water will be drawn under Company arrangements from Bn.H.Q. in petrol Tins.

In the Field,
11.8.17.

John E Rowbotham
Major,
8/7th Bn. Manchester Regt.

SECRET. Copy No 14

2/7th Battalion Manchester Regiment Order No.32.

Ref. FURNES, 1.40000,
Provisional Issue.

In the Field, 26.8.17.

1. **RELIEF.** The Battalion will relieve the 1/7th Bn. Duke of Wellingtons West Riding Regiment, in Coast Defence at LA PANNE, to-morrow 27.8.17.

2. **DISTRIBUTION.** LEFT Front Line Defence. "C" Coy. (Posts S,T,U,V).
RIGHT " " " "A" " (Posts N,O,P,Q,R).
RESERVE in Billets, "B" and "D" Coys.

3. **GUIDES AND ORDER OF MARCH.** Guides will meet Companies on Coast Road at M.9.a.9.0. at 3-45 a.m.
Companies will move in the following order:- "C" "A" "B" "D" "H.Q", first Company passing Starting Point at 4-30 a.m., others following at intervals of 5 minutes. An interval of 200 yards will be kept between Platoons.

4. **DRESS.** F.S.M.O. Steel Helmets will be worn.

5. **STARTING POINT.** M.6.a.25.80.

6. **TRANSPORT AND Q.M.STORES.** The Transport Officer will arrange for a Limber to report to each Coy.H.Q. at 6-30 p.m. to-night to load up with Lewis Guns etc. These will be parked near Bn.H.Q. for the night.
Officers Valises and Company Stores will be at Q.M. Stores ready for loading at 4-0 a.m.
Q.M.Stores will remain in present position.

7. **RATIONS.** Part Rations will be issued to Companies at 8-0 p.m. to-night. The remainder will be carried on the Cookers.

8. **TRENCH STORES.** All Trench Stores, Maps, Defence Schemes, Detail of Work in progress, reports required etc. will be taken over, and copies of receipts forwarded to Bn.H.Q. by 10-0 a.m. 27.8.17.

9. **BILLETS.** O's C.Coys. will finally inspect Billets before moving off and render certificate to Bn.H.Q. that all Billets and vicinity thereof have been left clean and in good order.

10. **LOCATION.** O's C.Coys. will send in location of Coy.H.Q. immediately on arrival in Billets.

11. **COMPLETION OF RELIEF.** Completion of Relief will be reported by Runner.

12. **ACKNOWLEDGE.**

(Sgd) Arthur Smithies,
Lieut. & A/Adjt.
2/7th Bn. Manchester Regiment.

Issued at 6-30 p.m.

Copy No.1. Retained.
2. 199th Inf.Bde.
3. 1/7th West Riding Regt.
4. O.C.A.Coy.
5. O.C.B.Coy.
6. O.C.C.Coy.
7. O.C.D.Coy.
8. O.C.HQ.Coy.
9. T.O.
10. Q.M.
11. M.O.
12. R.S.M.
13. War Diary.
14. " "
15. " "

[illegible] Copy No ..14.......

CORRIGENDA TO

2/7th Battalion Manchester Regiment Order No.34.

Para.1. Line 2. For 5-45 a.m. Read 7-45 a.m.

Line 5. For 4-50 a.m. Read 6-50 a.m.

Para.4. Line 6. For 4-0 a.m. Read 6-0 a.m.

Para.8. Line 4. For 10-0 a.m. Read 12 noon.

ACKNOWLEDGE.

(Sgd) Arthur Smithies,
Lieut. & A/Adjt.
2/7th Bn. Manchester Regiment.

Issued at 7m15 p.m.

SECRET. Copy No. 14

2/7th BATTALION MANCHESTER REGIMENT. ORDER No 35.

Ref. Map 1/20,000 and 1/10,000 NIEUPORT Sheet 11.S.E. Sheet 12.S.W. 1.

In the Field. 20/8/17.

1. RELIEF. The Battalion will be relieved by the 2/6th Bn. Lancashire Fusiliers, on the night 21/22nd August 1917, and will go into billets in COXYDE BAINS (W.6.b.2/8)
The Quarter-Master's Stores and Transport Lines will remain as at present.
Companies will be relieved as follows:-
"A" Coy. 2/7 by "D" Coy 2/6th Lancs, Fus.
"B" " " " "C" " " " "
"C" " " " "A" " " " "
"D" " " " "B" " " " "

2. GUIDES. Guides - 1 per platoon (2 for H.Q.Coy) will meet incoming Battalion at the Transport Dump (M 25.d.00.50) at 9.0 p.m. on 21.8.17.
The relieving Battalion will march in the following order:- "D". "C". "A". "H.Q". "B"
Guides will report at Battalion Headquarters, before going out to the rendezvous, for cards.

3. ROUTE. "C" and "D" Coys, will move out by M.21.c.40/30 PAUE ROAD- OOST DUNKERQUE - OOST DUNKERQUE BAINS - COXYDE BAINS.
"A" "B" and "H.Q" Coys. will move by BOCHE AVENUE - SANDY TRACK - OOST DUNKERQUE BAINS - COXYDE BAINS.
These routes are not obligatory.
In the case of enemy shelling, Company and platoon Commanders may use their own discretion.
ROUTES should be reconnoitred beforehand.

4. TRANSPORT. The Transport Officer will arrange for the Lewis Gun Limbers of "C" and "D" Companies to be at the Transport Dump (M.25 d.00/50) facing W. at 11-30 p.m. on 21/8/17. and 2 L.G.Limbers of "A" and "B" Companies and a limber for H.Q. Coy, to be at pt.R.30.a.40/40 at the Sandy Track, facing W. at 11-30.p.m. on 21/8/17.
The Transport Officer will arrange for two limbers to stand fast at the Ration Dump tonight until ration parties return. This party should take with them all surplus kit possible.

5. BILLETS. Lieut. Morris, Sergt. Crompton and 4 C.Q.M.S's will report at H.Q.2/6th Bn.Lancs.Fus.COXYDE BAINS (W.6.b.2/8) at 9.0 p.m. on 21/8/17 for the purpose of taking over billets. They will meet their Companies at pt.X.1.a.15/95, the entrance to COXYDE BAINS, and guide them to their billets.

6. HANDING OVER. Companies will hand over all S.A.A., Bombs, Grenades etc., in the trenches, taking particular care that the amounts are correct. Attention is called to the orders already issued with reference to aeroplanes photographs and A.A. sights for Lewis Guns.
Copies of Stores handed over to be forwarded to Bn.H.Q by 12-0 noon on 22/8/17 without fail.

7. SANITATION. Latrines, Trenches, dug-outs etc., will be left scrupulously clean.

8. COMPLETION OF RELIEF. Completion of relief will be notified to this office by code letter "A"

A C K N O W L E D G E.

(Sgd) JOHN A. SCHOLFIELD. Captain.
Adjutant. 2/7th Bn.Manchester Regiment.

P. T. O.

DISTRIBUTION.

Issued at 3.0.p.m.

Copy No 1 Retained.
" " 2. 199th Bde.
" " 3. 2/6th Bn.Lancs. Fus.
" " 4. @ i/c Detachment,2/7th Bn.Manch.R.
" " 5. H.Q.Coy.
" " 6. "A" Coy.
" " 7. "B" "
" " 8. "C" "
" " 9. "D" "
" " 10. Medical Officer.
" " 11. Quarter-Master.
" " 12. Transport Officer.
" " 13. R.S.M.
" " 14. War Diary.
" " 15 " "
" " 16. " "
" " 17. Filed.

CONFIDENTIAL

ORIGINAL

Vol 7

WAR DIARY

OF

2/7 Bn MANCH REGT

from 1.9.17 to 30.9.17

VOLUME VII

APPENDIX

1. OPERATION ORDERS
2. CASUALTY RETURNS
3. MAPS.

Instructions regarding War Diaries and Intelligence Summaries are contained in F. S. Regs., Part II. and the Staff Manual respectively. Title Pages will be prepared in manuscript.

WAR DIARY
or
INTELLIGENCE SUMMARY
(Erase heading not required.)

Army Form C. 2118.

Place	Date	Hour	Summary of Events and Information	Remarks and references to Appendices
La PANNE	2/9/17	5-0PM	Operation Order No 37 issued Bn relieved in Coast Defence by 3/5th Bn Lanc Fus.	JHS
ST IDESBALD	3/9/17	10·AM	Bn goes into Reserve Camp at St IDESBALD	JHS
	3/9/17 to 19/9/17		Bn and Bde Training	JHS
OOST" - DUNKERKE	18/9/17	2PM	Operation Order No 38 issued Bde goes into line Bn in support in YORKSHIRE CAMP	JHS
			1 OR wounded on Working Party	
"	19/9/17		Bn finding working parties for R.E. and 10th D.C.L.I.	JHS
	19/9/17		1 OR wounded on working party	JHS
	23/9/17		1 OR wounded " " "	JHS
			Orders received for relief of 66th Divn by 42nd Div (1st Line)	JHS
	24/9/17	10AM	Operation Order No 39 issued Bn relieved by 1/6 Manchester Regt and proceeds to St IDESBALD	JHS
St IDESBALD	25/9/17	9AM	" " " 40 " Bn moved to GHYVELDE by road.	JHS
GHYVELDE	26/9/17	7PM	" " " 41 " Bn to move to RENESCURE 11 Anzac Corps Second Army on 28/9/17. Transport to go by road on 27/9/17 staying night at WORMHOUDT Bn will move by BUS	JHS JHS
BANDRINGHEM	28/9/17		Bn in billets (very scattered) in BANDRINGHEM. Training.	JHS

Major
Commanding 2/7 Bn Manchester Regiment

OPERATION ORDERS.

SECRET. Copy No ...15...

2/7th Battalion Manchester Regiment. Order No.37.

REF. FURNES, 1.40000, In the Field. 8.9.17.
Provisional Issue.

1. RELIEF. The Battalion will be relieved to-morrow, by the 3/5th Bn. Lancashire Fusiliers, and will move into Camp vacated by 2/6th Bn. Manchester Regt. W.10.b.4.6.

2. RELIEF TABLE.

2/7th Bn. Manch. R.	relieved by	3/5th Bn. Lancs. Fus.
"B" Coy.	" "	"D" Coy.
"D" "	" "	"B" "
"A" "	" "	"C" "
"C" "	" "	"A" "

3. GUIDES. Companies in the Line will provide a Guide for each post, other Companies 1 Guide per Company, to be at X Roads, W.15.a.2.7. at times as stated below:-

"D" Coy .... 10-0 a.m.
"B" " .... 11-0 a.m.
"C" " .... 11-10 a.m.
"A" " .... 11-20 a.m.
"H.Q" " .... 11-30 a.m.

A slip should be given to each Guide showing post etc. which he represents.

4. TRENCH STORES. All Trench Stores, Defence Schemes, Maps etc. will be handed over. Representatives from relieving Battalion will report to "H.Q" of Coys. in the Line about 9-0 a.m. to take over these Stores etc.

5. TRANSPORT. 1 G.S.Wagon will be at Q.M.Stores at 9-0 a.m.
1 " " " " " " " " 10-0 a.m.
1 " " " " " VILLA DES ACORES at 10-15 a.m. for Officers Kits etc.
One L.G.Limber will be at "A" Coy.H.Q. at 10-15 a.m.
" " " " " " "C" " " " 10-15 a.m.
" " " " " " "B" " " " 11-30 a.m.
" " " " " " "D" " " " 11-30 a.m.
All Transport except L.G.Limbers of "B" and "D" Coys. will move under orders of Transport Officer via KERKEPANNE leaving Transport Lines, LA PANNE, at 11 a.m.
L.G.Limbers of "B" and "D" Coys. by same route independently

6. MOVE. "A" "C" and "H.Q" Coys. will leave LA PANNE, W.15.a.2.7. at 5 minutes interval, starting with "A" Coy. at 10-30 a.m. and march via Coast Road to Camp.
One Officer per Company will be left to hand over Billets to incoming Battalion.
"B" and "D" Coys. as soon as relieved will march by same route to Camp.

7. BILLETS. Billets, dug-outs and posts will be handed over in a scrupulously clean and sanitary condition, and certificates that this has been done will be rendered to Bn.H.Q. by 5-0 p.m. to-morrow.

8. SANITATION. The Medical Officer will see that all Latrines etc. are left in a sanitary condition, and render certificate that this has been done to Bn.H.Q. by 5-0 p.m. to-morrow.

9. BILLETING. One representative from each Coy. and "H.Q" Coy. will report to Lieut.Morris at Bn.H.Q. at 7-30 a.m. and proceed to Camp W.10.b.4.6. to take over Camp etc.

10. COMPLETION OF RELIEF. Completion of Relief will be reported by O's C. "B" and "D" Coys. to present Bn.H.Q. by Runner.

(Sgd) Arthur Maithies,
2nd.Lt. & A/Adjt.
Issued at 5-0 p.m. 2/7th Bn. Manchester Regiment.

DISTRIBUTION.

Copy No.1. Retained.
2. 198th Inf. Bde.
3. 3/5th Lancs. Fus.
4. 2/9th Manch. R.
5. O.C. A. Coy.
6. O.C. B. Coy.
7. O.C. C. Coy.
8. O.C. D. Coy.
9. O.C. H.Q. Coy.
10. Lieut. Morris.
11. T.O.
12. Q.M.
13. M.O.
14. R.S.M.
15. War Diary.
16. " "
17. " "
18. Filed.

SECRET. Copy No ..12...

2/7th Battalion Manchester Regiment Order No.32.

Ref. OOXYDE AND LOMBARTZYDE, Sheets 1.20000.

In the Field, 18.9.17.

1. RELIEF. The Battalion will relieve the 9/5th Bn. East Lancs. Regt. in YORKSHIRE CAMP, to-morrow, the 19th inst.

2. ROUTE: Cross Roads W.18.c.3.7. - OOXYDE.

3. ORDER OF MARCH. "A" "B" "C" "D" "H.Q". First Company will move off at 2 p.m.

4. MOVEMENT. By Companies to OOXYDE, thence by Platoons. Usual distances will be observed.

5. HANDING OVER OF CAMP. Each Company will leave a rear party of 1 N.C.O. and 6 men to clean up Company Lines.
The P.M.C. will arrange for the cleaning of "H.Q" Mess.
2nd.Lt.J.H.Hodgkinson is detailed i/c of these parties.
He will hand over the Camp to the 2/5th Bn. Lancs. Fus. and obtain receipts for everything handed over, and on completion of duties will march the cleaning party to YORKSHIRE CAMP.

6. YORKSHIRE CAMP - ALLOTMENT OF COY. LINES. C.Q.M.S's will report at YORKSHIRE CAMP to-morrow at 10-30 a.m. to take over Company Lines, which will be allotted later to-day.

7. Q.M.STORES AND TRANSPORT. The Quarter-Masters Stores and Transport Lines will move in accordance with 199th Infantry Brigade Administrative Order No.10 already issued.
The Transport Officer will arrange for Lewis Gun Limbers also 1 Limber for "H.Q" (A) Coy. to report to Companies ½ an hour before times for moving off.
Officers Valises and blankets in bundles of 10 and properly labelled, will be stacked at Q.M.Stores by 10 am.

8. WORKING PARTIES. The following working parties will be found to-morrow:-

No. of men.	Working for.	Rendezvous and time.	Nature of Work.
1 Offr. & 70 O.R's.	10th D.C.L.I.	LAITERIE. 7-0 a.m.	35 BATH AVENUE. 35 BLIGHTY "

"A" and "B" Coys. will each find 35 Other Ranks for this work, and "A" Coy. the Officer. The party will move off from Camp at 5-0 a.m.

No. of men.	Working for.	Rendezvous and time.	Nature of Work.
1 Offr. & 70 O.R's.	10th D.C.L.I.	LAITERIE. 2-0 p.m.	35 BATH AVENUE. 35 BLIGHTY "

"C" and "D" Coys. will each find 35 Other Ranks for this work, and "C" Coy. the Officer. The party will move off from Camp at 12 Noon.

9. BOMBERS. 2nd.Lt.D.Morris will detail three Bombers to report to Sgt Parkin at Brigade Headquarters at 8-0 a.m. to-morrow.

10. Completion of Relief will be reported to Bn.H.Q. by Runner.

11. ACKNOWLEDGE.

(Sgd) John A.Scholfield,
Capt. & Adjt.
2/7th Bn. Manchester Regiment.

Issued at 2 p.m.

Copy No.1. Retained. No.2. 199th Inf.Bde. No.3. 2/5th E.L.Regt.
4. 2/5th L.F. 5. 2nd in Command. 6. O.C.A.Coy.
7. O.C.B.Coy. 8. O.C.C.Coy. 9. O.C.D.Coy.
10. O.C.H.Q.Coy. 11. T.O. 12. Q.M.
13. M.O. 14. P.M.C. 15. 2nd.Lt.Morris.
16. War Diary. 17. War Diary. 18. War Diary.
19. R.S.M.

SECRET. Copy No......14

2/7th Battalion Manchester Regiment Order No.~~42~~.39

In the Field, 24.9.17.

1. RELIEF. The Battalion will be relieved by the 1/6th Bn. Manchester Regiment to-day, and on relief will proceed to ST. IDESBALDE and occupy the same Camp vacated on 19.9.17.

2. ROUTE. OOST DUNKERKE - COXYDE BAINS INFANTRY TRACK - COXYDE BAINS - ST. IDESBALDE.

3. ORDER OF MARCH. "A" "B" "C" "D" "H.Q". The Band will parade with "B" Coy. "A" Coy. will move off at 2 p.m.

4. MOVEMENT. By Platoons at intervals of 100 yards.

5. STORES. Officers Kits and Blankets, rolled in bundles of 10 and properly labelled, will be dumped outside the Q.M.Stores not later than 10 a.m.

6. REAR PARTY. Reference preliminary Order issued 23.9.17, para.5.
   For 2nd.Lt.D.Morris. Read 2nd.Lt.A.G.Aldred.

7. WORKING PARTIES.
   (a) 2nd.Lt.R.W.Fox and 61 Other Ranks now working for 184th (T) Coy.R.E. will join the Battalion at GHYVELDE on 26.9.17.
   (b) 2nd.Lt.A.Tarver and 52 Other Ranks now working for XV Corps H.A. will join the Battalion at ST. IDESBALDE, before 5-30 p.m. on 25.9.17.
   Both these parties will bring away with them rations for the day following the day of reporting to the Battalion.

8. TRANSPORT. The Transport Officer will arrange for Lewis Gun Limbers and 1 Limber for "H.Q" (A) Coy. to report to their respective Companies at 1 p.m. to-day.

9. SANITATION. All Hutments, Cookhouses etc. will be left in a scrupulously clean condition.

10. Completion of Relief will be immediately reported to Bn.H.Q. by runner.

11. ACKNOWLEDGE.

(Sgd) John A.Scholfield,
Capt. & Adjt.
2/7th Bn. Manchester Regiment.

Issued at 10 a.m.

Copy No.1. Retained.
2. 199th Inf.Bde.
3. 1/6th Manch. R.
4. 2nd in Command.
5. O.C.A.Coy.
6. O.C.B.Coy.
7. O.C.C.Coy.
8. O.C.D.Coy.
9. O.C.H.Q.Coy.
10. T.O.
11. Q.M.
12. M.O.
13. R.S.M.
14. War Diary.
15. " "
16. " "
17.

SECRET. Copy No ....

2/7th Battalion Manchester Regiment Order No.48.

COXYDE, Sheet 1.20000.
FURNES, 1.40000.

In the Field, 25.9.17.

1. MOVE. The Battalion will move from ST. IDESBALDE to GHYVELDE to-day.

2. ORDER OF MARCH. Parade will be ready to march off at 3-30 p.m. in the following order:- "H.Q" "A" "B" "C" "D", "A" Transport, "B" Transport.

3. ROUTE. Cross Roads W.18.c.5.7. - KERKEPANNE - LA PANNE - ADINKERKE - GHYVELDE.

4. MOVEMENT. A distance of 200 yards will be observed between Companies and between "A" and "B" Transport.

5. STORES. Baggage and Supply Wagons will move with the 544 Coy. A.S.C. at 7-30 a.m. to-day.
A motor lorry will be at the disposal of the Quarter-Master at 10 a.m.
Officers Kits will be stacked outside the Quarter-Masters Stores by 9-0 a.m. and will be loaded in the lorry.
The Transport with regulation loads will be ready packed by 12 Noon.

6. SANITATION. Every effort will be made to clean up the Camp before evacuation.

7. ACKNOWLEDGE.

(Sgd) John A.Scholfield,
Capt. & Adjt.
2/7th Bn. Manchester Regiment.

Issued at 9 a.m.

Copy No.1. Retained.
2. 199th Inf.Bde.
3. 2nd in Command.
4. O.C.A.Coy.
5. O.C.B.Coy.
6. O.C.C.Coy.
7. O.C.D.Coy.
8. O.C.HQCoy.
9. T.O.
10. Q.M.
11. M.O.
12. R.S.M.
13. War Diary.
14. " "
15. " "
16. Filed.

SECRET.   Copy No ..12...

2/7th Battalion Manchester Regiment Order No 46.

Ref. Dunkerque 1a. 1/40,000   26/9/17
Hazebrouck 5a. 1/100,000.

1. TRANSFER. The [illegible] Division will be transferred from the IV Corps Area to II Anzac Corps Area, Second Army.

2. MOVE. The Battalion will move by bus from GHYVELDE to [illegible] Area on September 27th and 28th.

3. ADVANCE PARTY. 2/Lt. [illegible]orris will be placed in charge of the Advance party, composed of six N.C.O's (one from each Company and one from the Transport. They will report to this Officer at [illegible] a.m. at billet No.[illegible] on 27/9/17. Twenty Four hours rations will be carried.

4. TRANSPORT. The Transport Officer will report to Capt. Sandilands, O.C. [illegible] Coy. A.S.C., for orders to-day.
The Brigade Transport will form up on the GHYVELDE - LES MOERES road at [illegible] a.m. on Sept. 27th in the following order, [illegible] Coy. A.S.C. with the head at Cross Roads [illegible] 6.5.

Brigade Headquarters.
2/7th Bn. Manch. R.
2/[illegible]th Bn. Manch. R.
etc.

[illegible] yds. interval will be maintained between Units.
The Quarter-master Sergeant will report on arrival at halting point for the night to O.C. Column.
All cycles with riders will accompany the Transport.
A guide will be sent by 2/Lt. [illegible]orris to meet the Transport at cross roads near LE [illegible] at 11-0 a.m. [illegible] to guide transport to Billets.
Steel helmets will be worn.

5. [illegible]. Baggage wagons will be collected at [illegible] p.m today. One A.S.C. motor lorry will travel with the buses on [illegible]/17. The Quarter-Master will arrange loads Officers' Valises will travel in the motor lorry and will be dumped as laid down in Appendix "A"
The Quarter-master will arrange for each Company to draw sufficient dixies for cooking on 27th and 28th.

6. MOTOR LORRIES. Troops will be drawn up ready to embus at 10-0 a.m. on [illegible]/17.
Detailed arrangements for embussing are given in Appendix "A" which will be issued later.
O.C. H.Q.Co. will detail a guide to report at Brigade Headquarters at [illegible] a.m. on [illegible]/17 to guide motor lorries to the Battalion.
The Battalion will debus on the [illegible] - [illegible] road, near the windmill (under [illegible] in [illegible]) where Company guides will meet the Battalion and lead to billets.

7. DRESS. F.S.M.O. Each man will carry his blanket rolled under his pack. Steel helmets will be worn.

8. MARCH DISCIPLINE. Particular attention is to be paid to March Discipline.

9. WATER. In absence of the Water Carts the Medical Officer will arrange water supply.

10. ACKNOWLEDGE

(Sgd) John A. Scholfield,
Capt & Adjt.
2/7th Battn. Manchester Regiment.

Issued at 7-0 p.m.

Copy No 1 [illegible]
" " [illegible]
" " [illegible]
" " 4 [illegible] Co.
" " [illegible] " "
" " [illegible] " "
" " [illegible] " "
" " [illegible] Co.
" " [illegible]
" " 10 Transport Officer.
" " 11 [illegible]
" " 12 [illegible] Officer.
" " 13 [illegible]
" " 14 War Diary.
" " 15 " "
" " 16 " "
" " 17 Spare.

SECRET. APPENDIX "A" Copy No 12

to accompany

2/7th Battalion Manchester Regiment, Order No.43.

1. Embussing will take place on the main PONT DE GHYVELDE - DUNKERKE ROAD.

2. Buses and Lorries will debus B. Infantry Brigade, X. Division in GHYVELDE, and then proceed to embussing place to take up 199th Infantry Brigade.

3. personnel will be lined up on right side of the road ready to embus at 11-30 a.m. in groups of ½ platoons ~~[illegible]~~ 6 ½ platoons to 30 yards of road space, 1 Bus takes 25 persons, 1 Lorry takes 20 persons.

4. (a) The Brigade will embus in the following order, with the head at PONT ZUYDCOOTE.

Brigade H.Q.	4	busses.
2/5th Bn.Manch.R. ...	33	"
2/6th Bn.Manch.R. ...	31	"
2/7th Bn.Manch.R. ...	16	"
	22	Lorries.

etc.

(b) __ALLOTMENT OF BUSSES.__

		__Number.__
Commanding Officer.	Bus.	69
H.Q.Co.	"	70 - 73
"A" Co.	"	74 - 81
"B" Co.	"	82 - 84
"B" Co.	Lorry.	1 - 5
"C" Co.	"	6 - 13
"D" Co.	"	14 - 21
Spare.	"	22

5. Each Company will detail one guide per platoon to report to the Adjutant at 9-15.am. on 28/9/17.
Each Company will have two vehicles per platoon.
Guides will report with slips upon which will be written the numbers of the two vehicles which are allotted to their platoon.

6. All vehicles are numbered on the off side and numbers shown above must be strictly adhered to.

7. An Officer will ride on each bus.

8. Companies will parade in time to move off at 10-15.am.

9. All Officers' Valises, stores etc. will be stacked in the garden of H.Q.Mess, Billet No.24 by 8-0.am.
The R.S.M. will detail a carrying party of 1 N.C.O. and 20 other ranks to report to the Quarter Master at 7-30.am. for loading purposes. When the work is completed they will rejoin their Companies.

10. Appendix "B" shews place of embussment.

(Sgd) John A.Scholfield,
Capt & Adjt.
2/7th Battn.Manchester Regiment.

Issued to all in receipt of
Operation Order No.43.

CONFIDENTIAL

199/66

Vol 8

WAR DIARY

OF

2/7th Bn. MANCH. REGT.

VOLUME VIII

OCTOBER 1917

Page 1

Instructions regarding War Diaries and Intelligence Summaries are contained in F. S. Regs., Part II. and the Staff Manual respectively. Title Pages will be prepared in manuscript.

WAR DIARY
or
INTELLIGENCE SUMMARY
(Erase heading not required.)

Army Form C. 2118.

Place	Date	Hour	Summary of Events and Information	Remarks and references to Appendices
BRANDRINGHEM	1/10/17		Bn in training	JHB
"	2/10/17	9 PM	OPERATION ORDER No 42 issued for move to EECKE area	JHB
"	3/10/17		Orders suddenly changed Bn bussed to CAESTRE and entrained at 9 am 4/10/17 for	
"	4/10/17		BRANDHOEK area. Transport to go by road and to billet in CASSEL area	JHB
			OPERATION ORDER No 42 Cancelled.	
			9 Officers 164 OR proceed to Reinforcement camp	JHB
"	5/10/17	8 AM	Advance Party proceeded to E of Ypres in ZONNEBEKE-STADEN line	JHB
		9 AM	Bn proceeded to line on foot through YPRES bivouacked near MENIN GATE	JHB
"			Extra ammunition issued and Bn proceeded to take over line from 39th & 40th Australian	JHB
E of YPRES			Bns Right Firing line A Coy. Left Firing line B Coy	JHB
			Right Support C Coy. Left Support D Coy	
			Bn H.Q. Shell hole close to BEECHAM.	JHB
"	6/10/17	1 PM	Relief Complete in spite of heavy enemy Counter attack	JHB
			Lines shelled by enemy throughout the day increasing to intensity at night	
			Two Germans shot during the night by A Coy one killed & one wounded. Both brought in.	JHB
	7/10/17	5 PM	Bn HQ blown up by Boche Barrage which preceded Counter-attack	JHB

2449 Wt. W14957/M90 750,000 1/16 J.B.C. & A. Forms/C.2118/12.

Page 2

Instructions regarding War Diaries and Intelligence Summaries are contained in F. S. Regs., Part II. and the Staff Manual respectively. Title Pages will be prepared in manuscript.

WAR DIARY
or
INTELLIGENCE SUMMARY
(Erase heading not required.)

Army Form C. 2118.

Place	Date	Hour	Summary of Events and Information	Remarks and references to Appendices
E of YPRES	7/10/17	5.30 PM	Commanding Officer (Major John [illegible]) at Brigade [illegible] [illegible]. Situation handled by Lieut [illegible] Scout officer who [illegible] [illegible] organised reinforcements from [illegible] Bn 2/5 Bn [illegible] Regt. Attack driven off with heavy loss. Great lack of rations & water. Bn HQ removed to SPRINGFIELD	
"	8/10/17		Rations & water got up to the Coys after great difficulty weather conditions [illegible]	
"	9/10/17	5.20 AM	197th Infantry Bde attacked on our front - owing to weather conditions 2/5 [illegible] [illegible] were not in assembly trenches. CO [illegible] [illegible] orders to [illegible] [illegible] CEMETERY.	
"		6.30 AM	OC A Coy collected remnants and mopped up CEMETERY 19 prisoners taken	
"		6 PM	Heavy German Counter-attack [illegible]. Many stragglers from 197 Brigade were collected and absorbed into our FRONT LINE	
"	10/10/17	AM	Bn relieved in front line by 2/5 Bn Man Regt. The Bn [illegible] up position W of HILL 40. Rations and water issued	

2449 Wt. W14957/M90 750,000 1/16 J.B.C. & A. Forms/C.2118/12.

Page 3

Instructions regarding War Diaries and Intelligence Summaries are contained in F. S. Regs., Part II. and the Staff Manual respectively. Title Pages will be prepared in manuscript.

WAR DIARY
or
INTELLIGENCE SUMMARY
(Erase heading not required.)

Army Form C. 2118.

Place	Date	Hour	Summary of Events and Information	Remarks and references to Appendices
MENIN GATE	10/10/17	6PM	Bn proceeded to MENIN GATE to bivouac 10 officers 103 OR marched out Total Casualties whilst in line 2nd Lieut Young killed — 110 OR wounded (1 since died of wounds) 2nd Lieut Rudd wounded — 37 OR missing 42 OR killed In addition (approximately) 100 OR and 5 Officers evacuated sick etc	JHS JHS JHS JHS
BRANDHOEK	11/10/17	6AM	Bn proceeded by lorry to BRANDHOEK	JHS
ARQUES	13/10/17	9AM	Bn entrained at BRANDHOEK detrained at ARQUES to billets on the outskirts of the town	JHS
" "	14/10/17		Bn in training - reinforcements expected 3 OR reinforcements received.	JHS
" "	19/10/17		103 Reinforcements received	JHS
" "	21/10/17		70 " " 22nd 2/Lt R N Beasley reported for duty	
			29th " W Haslam " " "	
" "	23/10/17		12 " " 31st Lt M Cooper " " "	JHS
" "	28/10/17		1 " " 31st 2/Lt F Hale " " "	
" "	29/10/17	9PM	INSPECTION ORDER ISSUED for inspection by Commander in Chief	JHS

2449 Wt. W14957/M90 750,000 1/16 J.B.C. & A. Forms/C.2118/12.

Instructions regarding War Diaries and Intelligence Summaries are contained in F. S. Regs., Part II. and the Staff Manual respectively. Title Pages will be prepared in manuscript.

WAR DIARY
or
INTELLIGENCE SUMMARY
(Erase heading not required.)

Army Form C. 2118.

Place	Date	Hour	Summary of Events and Information	Remarks and references to Appendices
ARQUES	31/10/17	11 AM	Presentation of ribbands to the following Officers NCOs and men by G.O.C. 66th Div Extract from II nd Corps Routine Orders dated 20.10.17 "The Corps Commander, under authority delegated to him has awarded the Military Medal to the undermentioned NCOs & men	

UNIT	REGTL No	RANK and NAME
2/7 Bn Man Regt	277359	L/Corporal C. WHITTAKER
"	275708	Sgt W MOORE
"	42783	Pte A INSLEY
"	275288	Sgt S. JENNER
"	276905	L/Cpl P O'REILLY
"	275365	Cpl G. MOTTRAM
"	277085	Pte D.T LEWIS
"	44777 →	Pte C.O.H TODD
"	277113 →	Pte A MELLOR
"	275855	Cpl H VICKERS
"	277365	Pte W H GREGORY"

also from D.R.O dated 27 10 17 "Under authority delegated by H M the KING. the Field Marshal [illegible] Commanding in chief has made the following awards

2449 Wt. W14957/M90 750,000 1/16 J.B.C. & A. Forms/C.2118/12.

Page 5

Instructions regarding War Diaries and Intelligence Summaries are contained in F. S. Regs., Part II. and the Staff Manual respectively. Title Pages will be prepared in manuscript.

WAR DIARY
or
INTELLIGENCE SUMMARY
(Erase heading not required.)

Army Form C. 2118.

Place	Date	Hour	Summary of Events and Information	Remarks and references to Appendices
ARQUES	31/10/17	(continued)		
			Awarded the Distinguished Conduct Medal	
			Regtl No - Rank & Name - Regt - For gallantry on	
			277742 - Pte E. BILLINGTON - 2/7 Bn Man Regt - 7 Oct 1917	
			Awarded the Military Cross	
			Rank & Name - Unit - For gallantry on	
			2/Lieut J. M. HAYES - 2/7 Bn Man Regt att A.P.M. 66th Divn - 11 Oct 1917	
			Capt (A/Major) J. E. ROWBOTHAM - 2/7 Bn Man Regt - 9 Oct 1917	
			Lieut F M POTT - do - 7 Oct 1917	
"	31/10/17		Corrected casualties from YPRES operations: Killed & died of wounds / Wounded / Missing / Evacuated sick	
			Other Ranks: 46 / 116 / 4 / 107	
			Officers: 1 / 3 / nil / 4	JHS
"	31/10/17	6PM	Warning Order received that Bn will move to WALLON CAPPEL tomorrow 1/11/17	

W. Woodcock Lieut Col
Commanding 2/7 Bn Man Regt

2449 Wt. W14957/M90 750,000 1/16 J.B.C. & A. Forms/C.2118/12.

Copy No. 9..

2/7th BATTALION MANCHESTER REGIMENT INSPECTION ORDER.

Ref. Maps. Sheet 27)
" 36a) 1/40,000.

INSPECTION. 1. The Commander-in-Chief will inspect the Division on Monday October 29th 1917, commencing at 11-0am

DETAILS OF PARADE. 2. (a) The 199th Inf.Bde. will be drawn up in line on the north side of the main ARQUES - AIRE road, ready for inspection at 11-40.am.
The Battalion will have the 2/5th Bn.Manch.R. in front, and 2/6th Bn.Manch.R. in rear.
(b) The Battalion will be formed up in the BATAVIA CHATEAU grounds ready to move into position at 10-40.am. Company right markers will report to the Adjutant at the entrance to the Chateau grounds S.22 c 2.8 at 9-40.am.
(c) The Battalion will arrive at S 22 c 2.8. at 10-30.am.
(d) DRESS - TRENCH FIGHTING ORDER. Steel Helmets will be worn.
Box Respirators will not be carried.
Each Company will shew 152 other ranks on parade.

DETAILS OF INSPECTION. 3. (a) The Battalion will be in "In Line" with ranks closed. Bayonets fixed.
(b) An interval of two paces between Companies.
Ten paces between Battalions.
(c) Road junction will be left clear.
(d) All Officers, with the exception of H.Q.Staff will parade dismounted, and will conform in dress with the rest of the Battalion.
(e) All other Officers, with the exception of H.Q.Officers will stabd two paces in front of the centre of their commands.
(f) The Battalion will dress by the left, the leading section commander of each platoon acting as marker.

MARCH PAST. 4. (a) Immediately after the inspection, the Battn. will march past with Bayonets fixed. Distance as laid down in I.T.Sec.98.para.6 will be maintained

(b) The executive word of command "EYES LEFT" will be given by platoon commanders. All Officers will salute.

(c) The Divisional Band will play for the march past of the 199th Inf.Bde.

RETURN MARCH. 5. Troops will return direct to Billets after march past.

PARADES. (first) The Battalion will assemble in Line facing East with rear of the column opposite the Transport Lines at 7-30.am. in the following order:- Band, "A" "B" "C" and "D" Coys. This will be a dress rehearsal for the inspection parade. Every man who would attend the second parade will be there, and orders for dress etc will be the same as laid down for the inspection.
Company Commanders will arrange for their Companies to be ready on parade at 7-20.am. with each platoon sized.

(second) The Battalion will assemble in column of route with the head of Bn.H.Q. in the following order, Band, "A" "B" "C" and "D" Coys. facing South, in time to move off at 9-50.am.

NOTE. H.Q.COY. WITH THE EXCEPTION OF THE BAND WILL BE ON PARADE WITH EITHER "A" "B" "C" OR "D" COYS, AS THE CASE MAY BE.

A C K N O W L E D G E.

Issued to:-
199th Inf.Bde.
Second in Command.
"A" Co.
"B" "
"C" "
"D" "
"H.Q" Co.
R.S.M.
War Diary.
" "
" "
Spare.

(Sgd) John A.Scholfield,
Capt & Adjt.
2/7th Battn.Manchester Regt.

Parade States will be rendered to Bn.H.Q. at 8-30.am.

SECRET. Copy No 14...

2/7th Battalion Manchester Regiment Order No.42.

Ref. Map HAZEBROUCK 5a.
Sheets 27)
28A) 1.40000.

In the Field 1.10.17.

1. MOVE. The 66th Division will move from the RACQUINGHEM Area to the EECKE Area on 1st, 2nd and 3rd October.
2/7th Bn. Manchester Regt. will move to the EECKE Area (Western Sub-Area) on 3.10.17.

2. ORDER OF MARCH. Band, "H.Q." "A" "B" "C" "D", Transport "A", Transport "B".
Dress:- F.S.M.O. Steel Helmets will be worn.

3. STARTING POINT. Road Junction A.24.a.70.90. The head of the column to be at the Starting Point at 7-55 a.m.
A distance of 100 yards will be observed between Companies.
"A" and "B" portions of the Transport will move together.

4. ROUTE. PONT ASQUIN – X Roads B.3.b.9.0 – LYNDE – WALLON-CAPPEL – Road Junction U.24.c.2.0 – Level Crossing at LA BTE LOGE – Cross Roads at V.21.a.5.2 – Cross Roads V.22.b.0.8 – ST. SYLVESTRE CAPPEL.

5. ADVANCE PARTY. Advance party of 2nd.Lt.Morris and 1 N.C.O. from each Company will proceed to ST. SYLVESTRE on 2.10.17.
Rendezvous – Main Square WARDRECQUES at 8 a.m.
This party will report to Bn.H.Q. at 7 a.m. Dress:- F.S.M.O.
2nd.Lt.Morris will arrange with guides to meet the Battalion on arrival at ST. SYLVESTRE at 3 p.m. on 3.10.17, at X Roads P.35.b.5.8. to guide Companies to Billets.

6. OCCUPATION OF BILLETS. As soon as possible after arrival in Billets O's C.Coys. will forward to Bn.H.Q. lists of Billets occupied, also Sketch map shewing Billets and Company Alarm posts.

7. RATIONS. Haversack Rations will be carried on 3.10.17. Dinners on arrival.
Rations for 4.10.17 will be issued by the Quarter-Master on arrival in Billets.

8. STORES ETC. Blankets will be tightly rolled in bundles of 10, and dumped outside the Quarter-Masters Stores before 9 a.m. on 2.10.17.
Officers Valises will be dumped outside the Quarter-Masters Stores by 6 a.m. on 3.10.17.
The Quarter-Master will arrange for the packing of the two Baggage Wagons, which will accompany first line Transport, on 3.10.17, and the one and half lorries, which latter will be loaded by 3 p.m. on 2.10.17.

9. TRANSPORT. The Transport Officer will arrange for Travelling Kitchens to be collected from Company Headquarters in time for parade, and for the packing of Lewis Gun Limbers etc.
Company Mess Baskets will be loaded on the Travelling Kitchens

10. STORES – REMOVAL OF. On departure from [illegible], Companies will render a certificate to Bn.H.Q. that no Area Stores have been removed.

11. SANITATION. All Billets in RACQUINGHEM will be left in a scrupulously clean and satisfactory condition.

12. ACKNOWLEDGE.

(Sgd) John A.Scholfield,
Capt. & Adjt.
2/7th Bn. Manchester Regiment.

Issued at 9 p.m.

Copy No.1. Retained.
2. Booth Inf.Bde.
3. 2nd in Command.
4. O.C.A.Coy.
5. O.C.B.Coy.
6. O.C.C.Coy.
7. O.C.D.Coy.
8. O.C.H.Q.Coy.
9. I.O.
10. Q.M.
11. M.O.
12. 2nd.Lt.Morris.
13. R.S.M.
14. War Diary.
15. " "
16. " "
17. Filed.

4

199/66

CONFIDENTIAL 66

Vol 9

WAR DIARY

OF

2/7th Battn The Manchester Regt

From:- Nov 1st 1917 To:- Nov 30th 1917

Volume 8

Army Form C. 2118.

Instructions regarding War Diaries and Intelligence Summaries are contained in F. S. Regs., Part II. and the Staff Manual respectively. Title Pages will be prepared in manuscript.

WAR DIARY
or
INTELLIGENCE SUMMARY
(Erase heading not required.)

Place	Date	Hour	Summary of Events and Information	Remarks and references to Appendices
ARQUES	1/11/17	8.25 AM	Order No. 43 issued. Bn to move to WALLON CAPPEL area at 2.30 PM today	[illegible]
			Bn arrived. Coys very scattered. Bde at STAPLE. Bde Training to commence	[illegible]
STAPLE	7/11/17	6 PM	Bn HQ at le CHATEAU. Order No 44 and 45 issued for move to RENINGHELST area on the 9th. Transport to go by road on 8/11/17	[illegible]
EBBLINGHEM	9/11/17	3.45 PM	Bn entrained at EBBLINGHEM detrained OUDERDOM (BELGIUM) marched to camp (tents) arrived 7.30 PM.	[illegible]
WESTOUTRE			Orders received 12 midnight for move to YPRES area (Order No 46). Bn to move off at 8.30 am	[illegible]
YPRES	10/11/17		Bn in Reserve Div in line. 4 Coys detailed on working parties. Bn HQ Transport, QMstores behind	[illegible]
YPRES	20/11/17	11.0 AM	Order No 46 issued. Bn to move to YPRES BARRACKS in support. 1 Coy detached on working party YPRES	[illegible]
YPRES	22/11/17		Divn relieved in line by 49th Div. Bn moved from YPRES BARRACKS to posn in reserve	[illegible]
YPRES	24/11/17	9.15 am	Order No 47 issued. Bn to move to BERTHEN (FRANCE). Bn moved into billets there.	[illegible]
BERTHEN	26/11/17	8.0 pm	Order No. 48 issued Bn to move to CAESTRE AREA tomorrow at 11 am.	[illegible]
BERTHEN	27/11/17	11.0 AM	Bn arrived. Coys very scattered. Bde at CAESTRE. Bn HQ at LE PEUPLIER. Training.	[illegible]
BERTHEN	30/11/17		2nd Lt R.P. BROOKES reported for duty.	[illegible]
			CASUALTIES for month. 10 O.R. WOUNDED. Also 4 officers transferred	[illegible]

John E Rowbotham Major
Comdg 2/7th Bn Manchester R

2449 Wt. W14957/M90 750,000 1/16 J.B.C. & A. Forms/C.2118/12.

SECRET. Copy No. ..14.......

[illegible] Battalion Manchester Regiment ORDER No.[illegible].

Ref. [illegible] Sheet 27.

In the Field. [illegible]

1\. MOVE. The Battalion will move to the [illegible] area [illegible] today.

2\. MARCH TABLE.
(a) The Battalion will assemble in column of route with the head of the column opposite [illegible] facing the [illegible] road, in time to move off at [illegible] p.m. in the following order:- Band, "H.Q." "A" "B" "C" "D", Transport "A", Transport "B".
(b) Distances. 100 yards between Companies and between "A" and "B" portions of the Transport.
(c) Route. Road Junction S.17.c.70.75. - [illegible] - Road Junction T.10.c.0.7. - Cross Roads T.10.a.[illegible] - STAPLE.
(d) Guides. Guides of the billeting party will meet Companies at road junction T.11.c.[illegible] at [illegible] p.m.
(e) Dress. F.S.M.O. Steel Helmets will be worn. Mounted Officers will conform.

3\. BILLETS. The Brigadier-General, Commanding [illegible] Infantry Brigade hopes that all Companies will leave their billets and Transport Lines in the same clean and satisfactory condition as has always been the case with this Battalion.

4\. [illegible] [illegible]. The Quarter-master will arrange to convey the [illegible] of the Band. Sgt.Dmr.Kelly will arrange to dump these at the Q.M.Stores by 11 a.m.

5\. ACKNOWLEDGE.

Issued at [illegible] a.m.

(Sgd) John A.Scholfield,
Capt. & Adjt.
[illegible] Bn. Manchester Regiment.

Copy No.1. Retained.
2\. [illegible] Bde.
3\. 2nd in Command.
4\. O.C.A.Coy.
5\. O.C.B.Coy.
6\. O.C.C.Coy.
7\. O.C.D.Coy.
8\. O.C.H.Q.Coy.
9\. T.O.
10\. Q.M.
11\. M.O.
12\. R.S.M.
13\. Sgt.Dmr.Kelly.
14\. War Diary.
15\. " "
16\. " "

S E C R E T.

Copy No. 13

2/7th Battalion Manchester Regiment Order No 44

7th November 1917.

MOVE. 1. The Transport will move to MERE tomorrow.

2. The personnel of the Battalion will move to RENINGHELST. on the 9th instant.

3. Detailed orders for the assembly of Transport will be issued later.

4. The Transport officer will arrange for horses to fetch the Cookers from the Company Headquarters at 8-0.am. Two Cooks per Company will accompany the Transport.

5. Breakfasts will be at 7-0.am.

6. C.Q.M.S's will arrange to retain sufficient dixies to Cook Companies meals for the 8th and 9th.

7. Officers Commanding Companies will arrange that Lewis Guns and any drums and ammunition with the Companies shall be delivered by hand to the Transport Lines and packed on thelimbers by 8-30.am.

8. Two G.S.Wagons will be at the Quarter-Master's Stores for the conveyance of Stores.

9. C.Q.M.S's with requisite ration parties will draw rations for 9th inst at the Q.M.Stores at 11-0.am. NO LIMBERS AVAILABLE.

10. Orders for move of personnel and conveyance of blankets on 9th instant will be issued later.

ACKNOWLEDGE.

(Sgd) John A.Scholfield,
Capt & Adjt.
2/7th Battn.Manchester Regiment.

Issued at 6-0.pm.

Copy	No	1	retained.
"	"	2	199th Bde.
"	"	3	2nd in command.
"	"	4	O.C."A" Co.
"	"	5	" " "B" "
"	"	6	" " "C" "
"	"	7	" " "D" "
"	"	8	" " "H.Q"
"	"	9	Transport Officer.
"	"	10	Quarter Master.
"	"	11	Medical Officer.
"	"	12	R.S.M.
"	"	13	War Diary.
"	"	14	" "
"	"	15	" "
"	"	16	Spare.

SECRET. Copy No ......

2/7th Battalion Manchester Regiment Order No.45.

Ref. HAZEBROUCK 5a. In the Field, 8.11.17.

1. MOVE. The Brigade will move to WESTOUTRE Area to-morrow, 9th inst.

2. STORES. One Blanket will be carried on the men.
Cooking Dixies and all petrol tins will be carried to the Station by the Companies.
Remainder of baggage, i.e. the second blanket, Officers Valises and Company Stores will be stacked at the following places at times specified:-
All Baggage of "A" Coy. and "H.Q" (B) Coy. on road at "A" Coy.H.Q. by 8-0 a.m.
Baggage of "D" Coy. and "H.Q" (A) Coy. at road entrance to Bn.H.Q. by 8-30 a.m.
Baggage of "B" and "C" Coys. at ESTAMINET JEAN BART by 12 Noon.
Blankets to be in bundles of 10 and labelled.
Officers Valises with their Companies Baggage, as above.
C.Q.M.S's will be responsible that all baggage is stacked at stated times and one man per Company will be detailed to remain with baggage till it is loaded on the motor lorry.
The Quarter-Master will detail 1 N.C.O. and 4 men as loading party for each journey of the lorry.

3. GUIDES. The R.S.M. will detail a Guide to be at Brigade Headquarters at 7-45 a.m. to guide lorry to baggage dumps.
One guidealso must return with lorry on its return journey as guide to JEAN BART dump.

4. BICYCLES. All Bicycles will be returned to the Signalling Officer at 11 a.m.

5. ENTRAINING. Personnel will entrain at EBBLINGHEM and will be at the Station by 3-45 p.m.

6. STARTING POINT. Starting Point on Main HAZEBROUCK - EBBLINGHEM road at cross roads 800 yards N. of N. in WALLON CAPPEL.
Companies will pass starting point in following order - "H.Q" "A" "D" "B" "C" at 2-50 p.m., 100 yards intervals between Companies.

7. DRESS. F.S.M.O. with Blankets. Steel Helmets will be worn.

8. GUIDES. Guides will meet Companies at OUDERDOM at 6 p.m. and will guide Companies to Billets.

9. SANITATION. Especial care will be taken to leave Billets scrupulously clean as they will be handed over to another Division.
Usual certificates that no damage has been done will be obtained from billet owners.

10. SECOND MOVE. On 10th instant the following moves will take place:-
"A" Coy. complete will be permanently attached till further orders to 432nd Field Coy.R.E.
"B" and "C" Coys. will relieve two Companies of the 7th Australian Battalion on working duties, relief to be complete by 10 a.m. Further details will be issued later.
Battalion less "A" Coy. move to CANAL Area.
Bn.H.Q. at H.17.d.Central (Ref. BELGIUM, 28.N.W.)

11. ACKNOWLEDGE.

(Sgd) John A.Scholfield,
Capt. & Adjt.
2/7th Bn. Manchester Regiment.

Issued at 6 p.m.

Distribution over.

Copy No.1. Retained.
2. 199th Inf.Bde.
3. 2nd in Command.
4. O.C."A" Coy.
5. O.C."B" "
6. O.C."C" "
7. O.C."D" "
8. O.C."H.Q"
9. Q.M.
10. M.O.
11. R.S.M.
12. War Diary.
13. " "
14. " "

SECRET. Copy No. 14.

1/7th Battalion Manchester Regiment Order No. [illegible]

[illegible] [illegible]

1. The Battalion (less "A" Coy.) will move to the Infantry Barracks, YPRES (I.7.a. [illegible]) tomorrow 21.11.17.

2. Stores. All Blankets of "B.C" Coy. labelled and in bundles of 10, Stores and Officers Valises required at YPRES will be dumped outside the Q.M.Stores by 9 a.m.
The Quartermaster will detail loading and unloading parties.
"B" "C" and "D" Coys. will carry their own Blankets to Infantry Barracks, YPRES.
"C" Coy. and "D" Coy. will carry their own stores.
A Lorry will call at the Q.M.Stores at 9-15 a.m.
Rations for consumption on the 21st inst. will be delivered at the Q.M.Stores by the A.S.C. Time to be notified later.

3. Companies will leave their present quarters in time to arrive at Infantry Barracks, YPRES, at 11-45 a.m.

4. The Transport Officer will detail Transport as follows:-
Horses and 1 Limber to be at "B" Coy. cookhouse to take cooker and stores to Infantry Barracks, YPRES, at 11 a.m.
Horses at "C" Coy. cookhouse to take "C" Coy. cooker to Infantry Barracks, YPRES, at 11-15 a.m.
Horses at Bn.H.Q. to take "D" Coy. cooker to Infantry Barracks, YPRES, at 11 a.m.
1 Limber and Maltese Cart to be at Bn.H.Q. at 11 a.m.
He will also arrange to take Lewis Guns and 12 drums per gun of "B" "C" and "D" Coys. to Infantry Barracks, YPRES. These to be delivered at Infantry Barracks at 12 Noon.
Water Carts will be taken empty into YPRES, filled at the Watering Point there, and left at Bn.H.Q. Infantry Barracks at 11 a.m.

5. Huts and Billet Areas will be left in a scrupulously clean condition.

6. Completion of relief to be immediately reported to new Bn.H.Q. by Runner.

7. ACKNOWLEDGE.

(Sgd) John A.Scholfield,
Capt. & Adjt.
1/7th Bn. Manchester Regiment.

Issued at 12 Noon.

Copy No.1. Retained.
2. 127th Inf.Bde.
3. 1/5th Lancs.Fus.
4. 2nd in Command.
5. O.C.A.Coy.
6. O.C.B.Coy.
7. O.C.C.Coy.
8. O.C.D.Coy.
9. O.C.H.Q.Coy.
10. T.O.
11. Q.M.
12. M.O.
13. R.S.M.
14. War Diary.
15. " "
16. " "

SECRET. Copy No ....

2/7th Battalion Manchester Regiment Order No.47.

Ref. Sheets 27 and 28 **In the Field. 23.11.17.**
BELGIUM & FRANCE. 1.40000.

1. The Battalion will move to BERTHEN to-morrow 24.11.17.
(a) **Route.** H.19.d.8.2. - H.13.c.9.2. - ZEVECOTEN - RENINGHELST - WESTOUTRE (M.9.c.35.50) - M.6.c.1.3. - Cross Roads R.10.c. - BERTHEN.
(b) **Guides** will meet Coys. at BERTHEN and guide to Billets. Billet Area will be roughly R.27.b.and c. and R.28.a.and c.
(c) **Order of March.** Band, "H.Q" "B" "C" "A" "D" less 1 Platoon - 1 Platoon of "D", Transport.
(d) **Distances.** 100 yards between Coys. Band and "H.Q" will march with "B" Coy.
(e) **[illegible].** O.C."D" Coy. will detail 1 Platoon with an Offr.
(f) **Time of Start.** Leading Coy. will pass BELGIAN BATTERY CORNER at 8-15 a.m.
(g) **Dress.** Battle Order, Greatcoats rolled above the Haversack. Packs with Jerkins inside will be conveyed by Motor Lorry (vide para.3).
(h) **Meals.** Breakfast 6 a.m. Dinners on arrival.
(i) **Water Bottles** must be filled by 4-30 p.m. to-day.

2. **DETAILS FOR MOVE.**
(a) The R.S.M. will detail 3 cyclists (including 1 Signaller) to report to Lieut.Alfred at Area Commandants Office, BERTHEN, at 9 a.m. on 24.11.17. He will arrange for them to leave Camp at 7 a.m.
(b) The R.S.M. will detail 2 guides to report at Brigade Office at 6 a.m. to guide 2 motor lorries to Q.M.Stores. Capt.Edge will accompany the first lorry to BERTHEN.
(c) The R.S.M. will detail loading party of 1 N.C.O. and 4 Other Ranks to load and accompany **each** lorry. Not more than 1 N.C.O. and 4 men are to ride on each lorry.

3. **STORES.**
Baggage Wagons will be loaded at Q.M.Stores to-day and parked for the night in the Transport Lines.
Motor Lorries. All Baggage in Camp, Blankets, Officers Valises, and Packs (less Greatcoats) will be stacked by 7-15 a.m. at the Q.M.Stores. Packs containing Jerkins will be ready packed and marked to-night. Every pack will be marked with owners name and Coy. Marks not to show when pack is worn.

4. **TRANSPORT.**
The Transport Officer will arrange to have teams for Water Carts Kitchens, and Maltese Cart to be in Camp at 7-15 a.m., at which hour the above carts will leave Camp and join Transport at the Lines.
Officers will meet their Chargers on the march at the Battalion Transport Lines.

5. **REAR PARTY.**
Lieut.T.E.Brittain will stay in Camp i/c Rear party in accordance with this Office memo.C/92. 3 Other Ranks per Coy. will remain instead of the 4 mentioned in this memo.

6. **SANITATION.**
All Billets and Billet Areas will be left scrupulously clean, and reports will be handed in to B.O.R. by 7-30 a.m. by O's C.Coys. that this has been done.

7. ACKNOWLEDGE.

(Sgd) John A.Scholfield,
Capt. & Adjt.
Issued at 3 p.m. 2/7th Bn. Manchester Regt.

Distribution over.

Copy No.1. Retained.
2. [illegible] Inf.Bde.
3. 2nd in Command.
4. O.C.A.Coy.
5. O.C.B.Coy.
6. O.C.C.Coy.
7. O.C.D.Coy.
8. O.C.H.Q.Coy.
9. T.O.
10. Q.M.
11. M.O.
12. R.S.M.
13. War Diary.
14. " "
15. " "
16. " "

S E C R E T.

2/7th Battalion Manchester Regiment Order No 4[illegible]. Copy No 13

Reference Map
Sheet 27.

In the Field.
28th Novr.17.

1. MOVE. The Battalion will move to the CAESTRE AREA to-morrow.

2. MARCH ORDERS.
(a) STARTING POINT. Cross Roads R 37 d 30.35.
(b) ORDER OF MARCH. Band, "C" H.Q". "A" "D" "B" (less one platoon) - One platoon "B" Company.
(c) TIME. The leading Company will pass the Starting point at 11-0.am.
100 yards distance will be maintained between Companies. H.Q. Co. will march in rear of "C" Co.
(d) GUIDES. Guides will meet Companies at Road Junction W 3 a 6.5. at CAESTRE and guide Companies to billets.
(e) DRESS. F.S.M.O. with Jerkins strapped on the top of the pack.
(f) MEALS. Breakfast,. 6-45.am. Dinners will be taken on arrival.
(g) MOPPING UP PARTY. O.C. "B" Co. will detail one platoon as Mopping Up Party.
(h) ROUTE. Le ROSSIGNOL - THIOUHOCK - CAESTRE.

3. STORES.
(a) BLANKETS. rolled in bundles of 10 and correctly labelled, Officers' Valises and Company Stores will be dumped at the Q.M.Stores not later than 8-30.am.
(b) GUIDES. The R.S.M. will detail three guides to report to Brigade Office at 8-0.am. to guide three lorries to the Q.M.Stores.
(c) LOADING PARTY. The Quarter-Master will detail one N.C.O. and 4 other ranks to load, accompany, and unload each wagon.
(d) Captain H.Edge is detailed to accompany the leading lorry.

4. REAR PARTY. 1 N.C.O. and 2 other ranks per Company will report to Lieut.Hodgkinson, at Bn.H.Q. at 12-0.noon.

5. TRANSPORT. The Transport will move via METEREN and FLETRE at 10-30.am.
The Transport Officer will collect Cookers and Water Carts from Company H.Q. at 9-0.am. Two Cooks per Company will accompany each Cooker and prepare dinners en route.
A guide will meet Transport at CAESTRE and guide to billets.
Officers' mounts will be at Co.H.Q. at 10-30.am.

6. SANITATION. All billets will be left in a scrupulously clean condition, and certificates rendered to Bn.H.Q. by 10-30.am.

7. RUNNERS. On arrival at the new billet area each Company will detail a runner to report at Bn.H.Q. with the location of his Company.

8. ACKNOWLEDGE.

(Sgd) John A.Scholfield,
Capt & Adjt.
2/7th Bn.Manchester Regt.

Issued at 8-0.pm
Copy No 1 - retained.
" " 2 199th Bde.
" " 3 Second in Command.
" 4 - 8. Companies.
" No 9 Quarter-Master.
" " 10 Transport.Officer.
" " 11 Medical Officer.
" " 12 R.S.M.
Copies 13,14, and 15. War Diary.

CONFIDENTIAL

Vol 10

WAR DIARY

OF

2/7th Batt. the Manchester Regt

FROM: Decber 1st 1917 TO: Decber 31st 1917

VOLUME 9.

Army Form C. 2118.

Instructions regarding War Diaries and Intelligence Summaries are contained in F. S. Regs., Part II. and the Staff Manual respectively. Title Pages will be prepared in manuscript.

WAR DIARY
or
INTELLIGENCE SUMMARY
(Erase heading not required.)

Place	Date	Hour	Summary of Events and Information	Remarks and references to Appendices
CAESTRE AREA	1/12/17		Training. New area. Kitchens - rifle range - BF Course. Bombing grounds - latrines Horse Standings. All to be erected by the Bn. Difficulty over training grounds eventually overcome but work retarded	JHS
			Health of men good except for considerable number P.U.O	JHS
"	15/12/17	8 PM	Order No 49 issued for move of Bn to YPRÈS area	JHS Appendix I
YPRES AREA			C Company detailed in Infantry Barracks working under C.R.E 66th Divn attached to 49th Divn for rations etc	JHS
			A.B.D. Coys working under 430 432 & 431 Field Coys RE respectively Entraining at BRANDHOEK daily for work on II Anzac CORPS LINE 2/3rds strength working each day	JHS
"	30/12/17	3 PM	Order No 50 issued for Move to old billets in CAESTRE AREA on January 1st/18 Transport to move the day before.	JHS Appendix II
			Casualties during working party tour 1 OR wounded (shell fire) Strength of Bn on last day of Decr 1917 740 OR 38 Officers Ration Strength of Bn " " " " 558	JHS
			John E Rowbotham Major Commanding 2/7 Bn M/c Regt	

2449 Wt. W14957/M90 750,000 1/16 J.B.C. & A. Forms/C.2118/12.

R E L I E F   T A B L E.

Date.	Coy.	From.	To..	Guides.	Time and place.
Jan.18/ 19th.	H.Q.	West Farm Camp	Bn.H.Q.	1 O.R.	8-0.pm. I 11 b 1.7. Junction of HOLE TRACK and CAMBRIDGE ROAD.
"	"A"	"	Line Right.	1 Off & 1 O.R. per post. (total 5 O.R.)	
"	"C"	"	Line Left	1 Off & 1 O.R. per post (total 4 O.R.)	"
"	"D"	"	Support	1 O.R. per post and 1 O.R. for H.Q. (total 5 O.R.)	"
"	"B"	"	Reserve.	1 O.R. per pill box, and 1 O.R. for H.Q.(total 4 O.R)	"

Companies will move off in the above order.

S E C R E T.   Copy No 13...

I

2/7th Battalion Manchester Regiment Order No. 49.

Referemce Map
Sheet 27.

In the Field.
15th Decr.1917.

1. MOVE. The Battalion will move by lorry to-morrow to the RENINGHELST AREA (WINNIPEG CAMP).

2. STARTING POINT. The Battalion will be formed up in the following order:- "D" "C" "H.Q." "B" "A", with the head of the column facing ST.SYLVESTRE CAPPEL at road junction pt.Q 31 a 3.9. at 7-30am
Capt.J.Brown is detailed as Officer i/c embussing. He will arrange that 20 other ranks travel in each lorry, and that one Officer travels on the front of every lorry if possible. The convoy will move off at 8-0.am.

3. ADVANCE PARTY. Capt.J.Hodgkinson and one N.C.O. per Company will report at Brigade H.Q. at 7-0.am to-morrow morning.
Care will be taken that the Company representative meets its Company at the debussing point.

4. STORES - CONVEYANCE OF. The Battalion has been allotted three motor lorries and two Baggage wagons. These will be loaded at the Quarter-Master's Stores under the supervision of the Quarter-Master. The Divl. Train have arranged for the teams for baggage wagons to report at 7-0.am.
Any surplus baggage left behind will be dumped at the Stores and a responsible N.C.O. left in charge. The Quarter-Master will report on arrival at WINNIPEG CAMP to the Adjutant the amount of baggage left behind when arrangements will be made with the Brigade for its cartage.
The Signalling Officer will arrange for 7 other ranks to report to the Quarter-Master's Stores at 7-30.am to-morrow, who will be detailed to take bicycles. They will fall in with the Tansport and march with their bicyclesk
Officers' Valises and Company Stores will be dumped at the Q.M.Stores tonight. No Transport will be available in the morning.
BLANKETS WILL BE CARRIED ON THE MAN. STEEL HELMETS WILL BE WORN.

RATIONS. O's.C.Coys. should endeavour to take dixies and the necessary dry rations to make tea for the men on arrival at WINNIPEG CAMP. A good haversack ration should be issued.

5. TRANSPORT. The Transport will move to WINNIPEG CAMP under the orders of the Transport Officer, pulling out at 8-30.am.
Teams for Field Kitchens, Maltese and Mess Carts will report at the respective H.Q. at 7-0.am.
Route will be issued to the Transport Officer later.
One cook per Company will accompany the Field Kitchens on the march.
The Transport Officer will arrange for the Orderly Room limber to be at Bn.H.Q. at 6-0.am.

6. SANITATION. All billets will be left in a scrupulously clean condition. All temporary latrines will be filled in and all foul ground labelled as such.
The usual certificates that there are no outstanding claims for damage will be obtained from billet owners and forwarded to the Adjutant together with the certificate re state of billets.

7. LOCATION OF COMPANIES. On arrival at the new AREA Companies will send in the location of their Company H.Q. by runner.

A C K N O W L E D G E. (It has lately been noticed that acknowledgments of orders have not been carried out in all cases. The strictest attention must be paid to this.

Issued at 8.0 p.m.

(Sgd) J.N.Rostern Capt. & Adjt.
2/7th Battn. Manchester Regt.

Distribution.

Copy No.1 retained.
" " 2 199th Brigade.
" " 3 Second in Command.
" " 4 O.C. "A" Co.
" " 5 " " "B" "
" " 6 " " "C" "
" " 7 " " "D" "
" " 8 " " H.Q. "
" " 9 Quarter Master.
" "10 Transport Officer.
" "11 Medical Officer.
" "12 R.S.M.
" "13 War Diary.
" "14 " "
" "15 " "

S E C R E T. Copy No..13....

2/7th BATTALION MANCHESTER REGIMENT ORDER NO.80.

Ref.Maps, Sheets 27 and 28. In the Field. 30.12.17.

1. RELIEF. The 199th Brigade will be relieved at work in the Forward Area on Decr.31st 1917 and January 1st 1918.
The 2/7th Bn.Manch.R. will be relieved by the 2/6th Bn. Lancs.Fus.on Jan.1st 1918.

2. WORK. In order not to break continuity of work on Jan.1st 1918 the Battalion will carry on work on the day of relief. After work the Battalion will move to the same billets recently occupied round CAESTRE.

3. (a) An Advance party of 5 Officers from the 2/6th Bn.Lancs. Fus. will report to Bn.H.Q. on 31/12/17. They will each be attached to a Company. Also their batmen for accomodation.
(b) On the day of relief,1/1/18, the Officers attached to "A" "B" and "D" Coys. will accompany the respective Coy. to which they are attached to the Corps Line in order to reconnoitre and take every detail of the work in hand.
The Officer attached to "C" Co. will report to H.Q.,.R.E. LILLE GATE, YPRES, on 1/1/18 to get details of work.xxxxxxx
(c) All maps and sketches of the posts, defensive works and tracks will be handed over.
All sketches should be handed over by Officers in charge of jobs to that Officer of the advance party of the relieving Company who is going to take over the work.
(d) Before leaving work on the day of relief, Officers of the advanced parties will have explained to them in detail the necessary tasks for the following day, which should be laid out (as far as possible) before leaving work.
(e) All schemes for action in case of attack will be handed over.
(f) The C.R.E. is arranging to release "C" Co. from work in YPRES so that it can rejoin the Battalion at WINNIPEG CAMP not later than 4-0.pm on Jan.1st 1918.

4. MOVE. The Battalion will embus on the VLAMERTINGHE - OUDERDOM ROAD, opposite the Camp, in the following order on 1/1/18.
"C" "D" "H.Q" "B" "A"
Capt.J.Brown is detailed as embussing Officer.
The Battalion will embus at about 4-0.pm.
NOTE. The 2/6th Bn.Lancs.Fus. will arrive in the busses that will take this Battalion back to CAESTRE. O's.C.Coys will arrange to have half their hut accomodation vacated and ready for the new comers by 3-0.pm on 1/1/18.

5. HANDING OVER OF CAMP. The Camp will be handed over as far as possible with
1. Fires burning in all Officers huts,
Officers' Messes. Sergeants' Messes.
Q.M.Stores. Cookhouses.
2. A small supply of fuel for above.
The Area Commandant has been asked to send a representative to inspect the Camp the day the Battalion moves out. Every endeavour will be made to leave the Camp scrupulously clean. O's.C.Coys will forward certificates to Bn.H.Q. that their final inspection was satisfactory on arrival in the new billet area.

6. DEBUSSING. The Battalion will debus at ST.SYLVESTRE CAPPEL.

7. BILLETING PARTIES. O's.C.Coys. may make arrangements to send one responsible N.C.O. to CAESTRE tomorrow, 31/12/17.

8. BILLETING AREAS. Billeting Areas will be the same as those pretiously occupied by Companies.

9. MEDICAL ARRANGEMENTS. The sick, will, on and after 2/1/18 be dealt with by 2/2nd East Lancs.Field Amb. at CAESTRE.

10. TRANSPORT. The Transport will move on 31/12/17 to BOESCHEPEAREA (WEST) where it will stay the night, moving early on 1/1/18 to the old standings in the CAESTRE AREA. The Transport Officer will send a mounted Advanced party to report to the Area Commandant at BOESCHEPE for accomodation at least three hours before his transport will arrive. The Transport Officer will collect the 1 water cart (less petrol tins) the limber, and field kitchen of "C" Co's at YPRES today. "C" Co. will make arrangements to keep back sufficient dixies and petrol tins to carry them over the 31/12/17 and 1/1/18.

11. STORES ETC. Baggage and supply wagons will report to the Q.M.Stores today. These wagons will travel with the Transport tomorrow. Three mechanical transport vehicles will report to the Q.M.Stores at 2-0.pm on 1/1/18. The Q.M. will send one to the Infantry Barracks, YPRES, to collect the blankets Officers' Valises and Company Stores of "C" Co. This wagon will then return to the Q.M.Stores to be loaded completely. All Officers valises, Company Stores etc, will be dumped on the spare ground opposite the "Lancashire Lads" Teatre at 1-0.pm on 1/1/18.
Blankets will be carried on the man.
On arrival at CAESTRE Companies should arrange to dump their dixies and petrol tins which will have been carried on the motor lorries for the personnel and put a guard over them. On arrival in billets they will then send fatigue parties back to collect the stores.
RATIONS. Supply arrangements will be in accordance with 199th Bde. Administrative Order No.33 already issued to the Q.M.
TURNOVER OF IRON RATIONS. Iron Rations which will be issued from the Q.M.Stores on 31/12/17 will be issued to all ranks. The Iron Rations at present in their possession should be consumed and replaced by the new ones to be issued.

12. RUNNERS. Companies will arrange for Runners to report daily at new Bn.H.Q. at 7-30.a. He will remain on duty until 12-30.pm. and a relief sent at 1-30.pm. The 1-30.pm relief will remain on duty at Bn.H.Q. until Bn.Orders are issued.

ACKNOWLEDGE.

(Sgd) John A.Scholfield,
Capt & Adjt.
2/7th Battn.Manchester Regiment.

Issued at 3-0.pm.

Copy No.1 retained.
" " 2 199th Bde.
" " 3 Second in Command.
" " 4 O.C. "A" Co.
" " 5 " " "B" "
" " 6 " " "C" "
" " 7 " " "D" "
" " 8 " " H.Q."
" " 9 Quarter-Master.
" " 10 Transport Officer.
" " 11 Medical Officer.
" " 12 R.S.M.
" " 13 War Diary.
" " 14 " "
" " 15 " "

- CONFIDENTIAL -

Vol 11

WAR DIARY

OF

2/7TH MANCHESTER REGIMENT.

FROM 1ST JAN to 31ST JAN 1918

- VOL., XI -

Instructions regarding War Diaries and Intelligence Summaries are contained in F. S. Regs., Part II. and the Staff Manual respectively. Title Pages will be prepared in manuscript.

WAR DIARY
or
INTELLIGENCE SUMMARY
(Erase heading not required.)

Army Form C. 2118.

Place	Date	Hour	Summary of Events and Information	Remarks and references to Appendices
YPRES AREA	1/1/18	4.30pm	Bn moved to old billets in CAESTRE AREA	[illegible]
CAESTRE AREA	2/1/18		Training on company training grounds.	[illegible]
	3/1/18		C+D companies inspected in the attack by American General + his staff	[illegible]
			2nd Lt J. C. Sutton awarded the Military Cross. (New Year Honours)	[illegible]
			Warning order for move into forward area on 11/1/18 issued.	[illegible]
	5/8/1/18		Training on company training grounds. Work in improving the area	[illegible]
	9/1/18	6.0pm	Order No 53. issued for Bn move to. POTISZE AREA	[illegible]
	11/1/18	9.0am	Bn moved by bus from ST SYLVESTRE CAPPEL – KRUISSTRAAT + marched from there to POTISZE.	[illegible]
POTISZE AREA	12/1/18		66th Divn relieved the 49th in the line	[illegible]
		2.0pm	Bn relieved the 1/7th WEST. YORKS as Bn in reserve for Rt Brigade Sector, being in new Nissen Hutments at WEST FARM CAMP	[illegible]
	12/17/1/18		Bn on working parties. 290 O.R. per day. Casualties 1. OR Died of Wounds	[illegible]
	17/1/18	11.45pm	Order No 54. issued for Bn move into line	[illegible]
	18/1/18		Bn relieved the 2/8th MANCH in Rt Sector of line. A + C. Coys in front line. D in support. B in reserve	[illegible]
LINE	20/1/18		Inter-company relief. B relieved A. D relieved C	[illegible]
	21/1/18		Order No 55 issued for relief of Bn	[illegible]
	22/1/18		Bn relieved by 2/5th EAST. LANCS. + proceeded to VANCOUVER CAMP in DIVISIONAL Reserve Casualties during tour 2. OR wounded	[illegible]
VANCOUVER CAMP	23/27/1/18		Bn on working parties. All available O.R. per day. No Casualties	[illegible]
	27/1/18		Order No 56 issued for Bn move into line.	[illegible]
	28/1/18		Bn relieved the 3/5th LANC. FUS as Bn in support for Left Brigade Sector. H.Q. at ANZAC. Coys as separated	[illegible]
LINE	29/1/18		1. O.R. Wounded	[illegible]
	31/1/18		Lt Col N. A. Baillie Hamilton 1st Black Watch appointed to the command of the Bn	
			Lt Col W. J. Woodcock struck off the strength 28/12/17	

G. A. Baillie Hamilton Lt Col
Comdg 2/7th Bn [illegible]

2449 Wt. W14957/M90 750,000 1/16 J.B.C. & A. Forms/C.2118/12.

SECRET. Copy No 12

2/7th Battalion Manchester Regiment.

WARNING ORDER.

1. The Battalion will move into the Forward (POTIJZE) AREA on Jan. 11th 1918, and will relieve a Battalion of the 146th Brigade on the night of 12th/13th January.

2. In the meantime Company Commanders should make sure that establishment of Arms, Equipment, etc, is complete, and that all necessary arrangements are made preparatory to the move.

3. (a) The extreme importance of the position which the Division is about to take over, and the necessity for the most vigorous action in the event of a temporary hostile success, must be impressed on all ranks.
(b) The whole of the Front Line SYSTEM is to be held at all costs. If the enemy does succeed in penetrating into any part of our positions, he is to be ejected at once by immediate local counter attacks.

4. A C K N O W L E D G E.

A Smithies
Lt.& Asst.Adjt.
2/7th Bn.Manch.R.

Issued at ......

Copy No 1 retained.
" " 2 Second in command.
" " 3 - 7 Companies.
" " 8 Medical Officer.
" " 9 Transport Officer.
" " 10 Quarter-Master.
" " 11 R.S.M.
" " 12 - 14 War Diary.

S E C R E T.   Copy No.

2/7th Battalion Manchester Regiment Order No 5[illegible].

Ref.Maps, Sheets Nos.   In the Field,
27 and 28. 1/40,000.   9th Jan.1918.

1. RELIEF. The Battalion will move by bus from the CAESTRE SUB-AREA to the POTIJZE AREA, on Jan.11th 1918, and will relieve a Battalion of the 146th Infantry Brigade on the night 12th/13th Jan.1918.

2. MOVE. The Battalion will form up in column of route in the following order:- "A" "D" "C" "H.Q.(a)" "B" with the head of the column at pt.Q 31 b 3.4, facing N. on S.SYLVESTRE CAPPEL - CAESTRE ROAD, at 8-45.am. ready to embus at 9-0.am. DRESS:- F.S.M.O. STEEL HELMETS WILL BE WORN. Blankets will be carried on the man. Capt.J.Brown is detailed as embussing Officer. Busses, Nos.[illegible] - 41 (inclusive) are allotted to the Battalion. O's.Coys. will hand Company embussing strengths to the embussing officer at 8-45.am. at the above point.

3. ADVANCE PARTY. One N.C.O. per Company will meet Lt.A.C.Aldred outside Brigade H.Q. at 7-30.am. on the 10th inst. Rations for the 10th and 11th will betaken. Accomodation for the night 10th/11th will be provided by Area Commandant, POTIJZE AREA. These N.C.O's will meet their respective Companies at the debussing pt. Road N. of KRUISSTRAAT from H 18 d 0.6 to H 12 d 4.8 at 10-30.am. on the 11th to guide them to the billeting area.
The Billeting Officerwill send a guide back to report to Q.M. Caestre Area as soon as location of Q.M.Stores in new Area is ascertained. He will guide lorries to new Q.M. Stores at BELGIAN CHATEAU on the 11th inst.

4. TRANSPORT. Transport will move independently at 8-45.am. on the 10th inst, to WIPPENHOEK, via CAESTRE - GODEWAERSVELDE - ABEELE- Mounted Advanced party will report at least three houts before the arrival of Transport to Lt.Col.Mulliner, Area Commandant, WIPPENHOEK. A guide from Advanced party will meet Transport at Cross Roads L 36 c 7.7. (ABEELE) to guide them to the lines. Transport will move independently on Jan.11th from WIPPENHOEK AREA to take over Transport Lines from corresponding Unit of the 146th Brigade in H.23. Rations and Forage for the 10th and 11th will be carried.

5. BAGGAGE [illegible]. Baggage and Supply Wagons will report to Q.M.Stores on the [illegible] instant.

6. LORRIES. One lorry for conveyance of Baggage will report to Bde.H.Q. CAESTRE at 7-0.am. on 11th inst. This lorry will do two journeys. Q.M. will arrange to send a guide to Staff Captain's Office, CAESTRE at 6-45.am. on 11th inst to guide lorry to Q.M.Stores.

7. STORES. Company Stores and Officers' Valises will be dumped at Q.M.Stores by 6-0.pm on 10th inst. No Transport will be available. O.i/c.Signals will arrange for four other ranks to report to Q.M.Stores at 7-30.am. on 10th inst to take bicycles. The R.S.M. will detail two runners also for the same purpose. They will march with the transport.

8. AREA STORES. All Area Stores on charge will be handed over to Area Commandant from whom receipts will be obtained. Receipts to be forwarded to Bn.H.Q. by noon on 12th inst.

9. TRENCH & AREA STORES IN 49th.DIV. AREA. All Reserve Supplies, Ammunition, Trench and Area Stores will be carefully checked before being taken over, and receipts will be given. Copies of receipts will be forwarded to Bn.H.Q. by 6-0.pm. on 13th inst.

10. RUNNERS. As soon as Transport and Q.M"Stores have been fixed, the Q.M. will detail the two runners mentioned in para.7 to report to Staff Captain, Brigade Rear H.Q. Infantry Barracks, YPRES.

11. CODE. "Code Names" and "Station Code Calls" will be taken into use on arrival in Forward Area.

12. SANITATION. All billets will be left in a scrupulously clean condition. All temporary latrines filled in, and all foul ground labelled as such.
The usual certificates that there are no outstandings claims for damages will be obtained from Billet Owners and forwarded to Bn.H.Q. together with a certificate re state of billets.

13. ACKNOWLEDGE.

(Sgd) Arthur Smithies,
Lt.& Asst.Adjt.
2/7th Bn.Manchester Regiment.

Issued at 6-0 pm
Copy No 1 retained.
" " 2 199th Brigade.
" " 3 Second in Command.
" " 4 O.C. "A" Co.
" " 5 " " "B" "
" " 6 " " "C" "
" " 7 " " "D" "
" " 8 " " H.Q."
" " 9 Quarter-Master.
" " 10 Transport Officer.
" " 11 Medical Officer.
" " 12 R.S.M.
" " 13 War Diary.
" " 14 " "
15 " "

S E C R E T   Copy No 12

2/7th Battalion Manchester Regiment Order No 54.

In the Field,
17th Jan.1918

Ref.Map. Sheet 62. 1/40,000.

1. RELIEF. The Battalion will relieve the 2/6th Bn.Manch.R. to-morrow in accordance with attached table.

2. TRENCH STORES ETC. All Trench Stores, Defence Schemes, etc. will be taken over and receipts given. Copies of receipts to be returned to Bn.H.Q. by 2-0.pm. 19/1/18.

3. MARCH DISCIPLINE Strict March Discipline will be maintained. An Officer or N.C.O. will march in rear of each party to prevent straggling.

4. COMPLETION. Completion of relief will be reported by wire to Bn.H.Q. by code word "EYE".

5. CAMP. All huts and latrines will be left scrupulously clean.

6. A C K N O W L E D G E.

Lt.& Asst.Adjt.
2/7th Bn.Manch.R.

Issued at 11-45pm

Copy No 1 retained.
" " 2 199th Brigade.
" " 3 2/6th Bn.Manch.R.
" " 4 O.C. "A" Co.
" " 5 " " "B" "
" " 6 " " "C" "
" " 7 " " "D" "
" " 8 " " H.Q. "
" " 9 Quarter-Master.
" " 10 Transport Officer.
" " 11 Medical Officer.
" " 12 R.S.M.
" " 13 War Diary.
" " 14 " "
" " 15 " "

S E C R E T. Copy No. 12

IV

Ref. Map.
Sheet 28.
1/40000.

2/7th Battalion Manchester Regimnt Order No. 55.

In the Field.
21/1/18.

RELIEF. (1) The 2/7th Bn. Manch. Regt. will be relieved in the Line on Jan. 22nd. 1918 by 2/5th East Lancs. Regt., in accordance with table attached.

(2) One Officer per Front Line Company will remain behind with the incoming Companies and will stay until "Stand To" on the morning of Jan. 23rd. 1918.

TRENCH STORES. All Trench Stores, Defence Schemes, Work in progress, Reports Required, etc. will be handed over and receipts obtained. Copies of receipts will be returned to Bn.H.Q. by 9.am. 23/1/18.

MARCH DISCIPLINE. Strict March Discipline will be maintained. An Officer or N.C.O. will march in rear of each party to prevent straggling

COMPLETION. Completion of relief will be reported to Bn.H.Q. by code word "TONY".

A C K N O W L E D G E.

(Sgd.) J.N.Rostern.
Lt. & A/Adjt.
2/7th Bn. Manch.Regt.

DISTRIBUTION.

Copy No.1 Retained.
" " 2 199th Brigade.
" " 3 O.C. "A" Coy.
" " 4 " " "B" "
" " 5 " " "C" "
" " 6 " " "D" "
" " 7 " " H.Q. "
" " 8 Quarter Master.
" " 9 Transport Officer.
" " 10 Medical Officer.
" " 11 R.S.M.
" " 12 War Diary.
" " 13 " "
" " 14 " "
" " 15 2/5th East Lancs.Regt.
" " 16 O. i/c Details.

REF MAP
SHEET 28 1/40000

RELIEF of 2/7TH BN. MANCHESTER REGT. by 2/5TH EAST LANCS REGIMENT.

COMPANY.	FROM.	RELIEVED BY.	TO	GUIDES MEET 2/5TH EAST LANCS	AT	TIME	REMARKS
H.Q.	BN. H.Q.	H.Q.	VANCOUVER CAMP.	1. O.R	YORKSHIRE DUMP.	2.30. p.m.	PROCEED BY MULE TRACK, KIT AND KAT TRACK TO
C	SUPPORT.	D	do.	1. O.R. PER POST AND 1. O.R. FOR Coy. H.Q. (TOTAL 5 O.R.)	do.	2.30. p.m.	BIRR X ROADS. ENTRAIN BIRR X ROADS
A	RESERVE	B	do.	1. O.R PER PILL BOX AND 1. O.R. FOR Coy. H.Q. (TOTAL 4 O.R.)	do.	2.30 p.m.	(LIGHT RLY) 7.30. p.m. ARRIVE VANCOUVER 8.30 p.m.
D	LINE LEFT.	C	do.	1 OFFICER AND 1. O.R PER POST (TOTAL 4 O.R.)	do.	4.0. p.m.	PROCEED BY MULE TRACK KIT AND KAT TRACK TO BIRR X ROADS.
B	LINE LEFT.	A	do.	1 OFFICER AND 1. O.R PER POST (TOTAL 4 O.R.)	do.	4.0. p.m.	ENTRAIN BIRR X ROADS (LIGHT RLY.) 10.0. p.m. ARRIVE VANCOUVER 11.0 p.m.

Companies will move off in above order.
2/Lt. H.A. Shirley is detailed as Entraining Officer who will meet a Brigade Staff Officer at BIRR X ROADS at 7.0. p.m.

IN THE FIELD
21/1/18.

(Sd) J. N. Rastern
Lt + A/Adjt
2/7TH BN. MANCH. REGT.

Copy No 12

SECRET.

2/7th Battalion Manchester Regiment Order No 66.

In the Field,
27th Jan. 1918.

Ref. Map Sheet 28. 1/40,000.

1. RELIEF. The Battalion will relieve the 2/5th Bn. Lancs. Fus. to-morrow, Jan. 28th in accordance with attached table.

2. DEFENCE SCHEMES ETC. All Defence Schemes, Trench Maps, Details of Work in progress, and proposed etc., will be taken over and receipts given.
Copies of receipts will be forwarded to Bn.H.Q. by 9-0.am. on 29/1/18.

3. TRACKS. Tracks are allotted to the Battalion as follows :-
"P" TRACK, CORDUROY ROAD, CONNEMARA TRACK.
If these tracks are being heavily shelled it is left to the discretion of Company and platoon Commanders to use tracks other than those allotted.

4. MARCH. DISCIPLINE. Strict march discipline will be maintained. An Officer or N.C.O. will march in rear of each party to prevent straggling.

5. CAMP. All huts and latrines will be left in a scrupulously clean condition.

6. COMPLETION OF RELIEF. Completion of relief will be reported to Bn.H.Q. by code word "DAMNIT"

7. WORK. Work will be carried on after relief in accordance with attached table.

8. A C K N O W L E D G E.

(Sgd) A Smithies
Lt. & Asst. Adjt.
2/7th Bn. Manchester Regt.

Issued at 6.0. pm

Copy No 1 retained.
" " 2 199th Bde.
" " 3 O.C. "A" Co.
" " 4 " " "B" "
" " 5 " " "D" "
" " 6 " " H.Q.(a)
" " 7 Quarter-master.
" " 8 Transport Officer.
" " 9 Medical Officer.
" " 10 R.S.M.
" " 11 O.C. "C" Co.
" " 12 War Diary.
" " 14 " "
" "15 " "

R E L I E F   T A B L E.

SHEET 28.

2/7th Bn.Manch.R. will relieve 2/8th Bn.Lancs.Fus. as under.

Coy.	Relieve.	at.	ENTRAIN AT Vancouver.	Detrain Vincey, Potijze.	Guides.	Route.
"C"	"C"	Support.	[illegible]-0.am.	10-[illegible].a.m.	D 26 c 1.3 Right Bde. H.Q.	"F" Track ZONNEBEKE TRACK.
"A"	"A"	Thames.	"	"	"	"
"D"	"D"	Albania.	"	"	Garter pt.	"F" TRACK.
"B"	"B"	Garter pt.	"	"	"	"
H.Q.	H.Q.	Garter pt.	"	"	"	"

Companies will be formed up ready to entrain at [illegible]-45.am. in above order from front to rear.

The train will carry 2/8th Bn.Manch.R, 2/7th Bn.Manch.R. 100th L.T.M.B. in that order from front to rear.

Capt.H.Edge is detailed as entraining Officer.

WORKING PARTY TABLE.

Party.	Found by.	Strength.	Working under supervision of.	Nature of Work.	Rendezvous as arranged with R.E.Co.	Unit now finding.
2	"B" Co.	50	Field Co.R.E.	Support Line posts.	-	2/5th Bn. Lancs. Fus.
4	"D"	50	"	Zonnebeke Rd.	-	"

THESE FIGURES ARE EXCLUSIVE OF SUPERVISING OFFICERS AND N.C.O'S

2/7th Bn. Manch R.

WAR DIARY

1st FEB

TO

28th FEB

VOLUME XII

28th FEB 1918

WAR DIARY
or
INTELLIGENCE SUMMARY
(Erase heading not required.)

Army Form C. 2118.

2/7 Manchester

Vol 12

Instructions regarding War Diaries and Intelligence Summaries are contained in F. S. Regs., Part II. and the Staff Manual respectively. Title Pages will be prepared in manuscript.

Place	Date 1918	Hour	Summary of Events and Information	Remarks and references to Appendices
ANZAC	FEB. 1.		Bn in Support. Coys on Working Parties.	ASA
	2		Order No. 57 issued for Bn move into front line.	ASA
LINE.	3.		Bn relieved the 2/8th Bn MANCHESTER. REGT. in left sector of left Brigade. 'A' Coy Rt Front Line, 'C' Coy Left Front line 'B' Coy Support. 'D' Coy Reserve. Front line a series of posts partly constructed. Day garrison of 1. NCO & 3 Men relieved at dusk by night garrison of 1 NCO & 10 men, who brought up material & worked on the posts all night. The garrisons of the posts rested with the Support & Reserve Coys while off duty.	ASA
			One coy of 2/8th Bn MANCH. R. attached to Bn for work & tactical purposes.	ASA
	3/9		Bn in line. Casualties 1. OR KILLED. 2. OR WOUNDED. No cases of TRENCH FEET.	ASA
	6.		2/LT. FREEMAN, 2/LT M.P.J. GAPP joined the Bn	ASA II
	8		Order No. 58 issued for relief of Bn	ASA
	9		Bn relieved by 5th Bn BORDER. R. 151st INF. BDE. & moved to DRAGOON. CAMP. POTIJZE.	ASA
POTIJZE	10		Bn moved by light railway to VANCOUVER CAMP	ASA
VANCOUVER AREA.	11		Bn marched, in accordance with order No. 59, to Divl Concentration Area, & was inspected on the march by G.O.C. Division. Bn in SCHOOL CAMP PROVEN. AREA.	ASA III
PROVEN AREA.	11		277794. R.S.M. JACKSON. W.J., 275407 A/L/SGT. PARKIN. E. awarded the CROIX de GUERRE (BELGIAN)	ASA
	12		Bn in training. Drill, Musketry, Bayonet Fighting.	ASA
	12		Draft of 10 Officers & 217 O.R. received from 2/8th Bn MANCH. R.	ASA VIII
	13/16		~~Training~~ [illegible] O.R received from H. B[illegible]	ASA
	17	4 35 pm	Order No. 60. issued for Bn move to HARBONNIERS AREA	ASA IV
	18	1. am	Bn entrained at PROVEN & detrained at GUILLICOURT & marched to billets at BAYONVILLIERS. B Coy acted as loading party for the Brigade & proceeded on the 2nd train at 4. am	ASA
HARBONNIERS AREA.	19/21		Training	ASA
	22		A Coy moved to VILLIERS. CARBONNEL to construct Divisional Staging Camp.	ASA
	23		Training	ASA
		10 45 pm	Order No. 61 issued for Bn move to VILLIERS CARBONNEL	ASA
	24		Bn marched to VILLIERS CARBONNEL & spent the night under canvas.	ASA I

Army Form C. 2118.

* Instructions regarding War Diaries and Intelligence Summaries are contained in F. S. Regs., Part II. and the Staff Manual respectively. Title Pages will be prepared in manuscript.

WAR DIARY
or
INTELLIGENCE SUMMARY

(Erase heading not required.)

Place	Date 1918	Hour	Summary of Events and Information	Remarks and references to Appendices
VILLERS CARBONNEL	FEB 25		Bn marched to HANCOURT in accordance with Operation Order No 62.	[illegible] VI
HANCOURT	26	7.5 pm	Order No 63 issued for Bn move into line	[illegible] VIII
	27		Bn marched to VENDRELLES & relieved the 8th Bn R.W. KENT R. 72nd INF BDE as Bn in reserve VILLERET SECTOR	[illegible]
VENDRELLES	28		Bn at work cleaning village & camp improvements.	[illegible]
			Strength of Battalion 54 Off. 930 OR	
			— do — (Ration) 36 Off 744 OR	
		3.30 pm	ALARM ACTION received Bn Standing to	

R. M. Baillie Hamilton Lt Col
Comdg 2/7th Bn Manchester R

2449 Wt. W14957/M90 750,000 1/16 J.B.C. & A. Forms/C.2118/12.

War Diary

Reference Battalion Operation Order No.50 :- The following points will be carefully observed.

1. Steel helmets will be worn and rifles slung over right shoulder.

2. Eyes right()orleft) by platoons, Officers saluting with right hand.

3. All Signallers will march in a formed body in front of Battalions.

4. prescribed halts will be observed with the exception of the halt at 9-50 which will be for 15 minutes (9-50.am. to 10-5.am.) to allow for correction of any mistakes in intervals.

5. Bands will play om the march.

6. All sick and unfit men should be disposed od before marching to-morrow.

7. The oder of march of transport will be as follows:-

10 Limbers.
2 Water Carts.
4. Trav.Kitchens.
1. Maltese Cart.
1. Officer's Mess Cart.
2 Bagage Wagons.

(Sgd.) A.Smithies.
Lt. & Asst.Adjt.
2/7th Bn.Manch.R.

Bn.H.Q.
10/2/18.

199th Brigade.
66th Division.

2/7th BATTALION

MANCHESTER REGIMENT

M A R CH 1 9 1 8

199
66.

CONFIDENTIAL

WAR DIARY OF

2/7th Bn MANCHESTER REGT

FROM:- MARCH 1st 1918 TO:- MARCH 31st 1918

(VOLUME)

——— o ———

Instructions regarding War Diaries and Intelligence Summaries are contained in F. S. Regs., Part II. and the Staff Manual respectively. Title Pages will be prepared in manuscript.

WAR DIARY
or
~~INTELLIGENCE SUMMARY~~
(Erase heading not required.)

Army Form C. 2118.

Place	Date	Hour	Summary of Events and Information	Remarks and references to Appendices
VENDELLES	1/3/18		Bn in reserve	[illegible]
		11.50pm	Order No 64 issued for move into line	[illegible]
	2/3/18		Bn relieved 2/6th Bn MANCH R as Bn in Support ~~[illegible]~~ HQ at [illegible] WOOD, B C & D Coys in RED LINE A Coy in Support	[illegible]
LINE	2/6.3.18		Bn in support. Casualties for tour 1 OR [illegible] 1 OR [illegible]	[illegible]
	6.3.18		Bn after relief in Support by 2/5th Bn MANCH R, relieved the 2/6th Bn MANCH R in the line as per Order No 65	[illegible]
			A. B & D. Coys in front line. C Coy in VILLERET [illegible] HQ [illegible]	[illegible]
	6/14.3.18		Bn in line. Work on [illegible] Posts [illegible] for Support [illegible] Casualties for tour 2 OR wounded	[illegible]
	14.3.18		Bn relieved by 2/5th Bn MANCH R [illegible] RT SUPPORT. HQ and MONTIGNY. C Coy in RED LINE. D Coy JEANCOURT [illegible] platoon at BROSSE WOOD No 1 A & B. Coys at MONTIGNY	[illegible]
		11.50pm	Order received "MAN BATTLE POSITIONS". On which D Coy [illegible] RED LINE, HQ [illegible] to BROSSE WOOD No 1 B Coy to JEANCOURT	[illegible]
	15.3.18	7 AM	Order "RESUME NORMAL CONDITIONS" received, when Bn returned [illegible]	[illegible]
	16.3.18		Orders for raid issued. B Coy practised raid at MONTIGNY	[illegible]
	18.3.18	12.30AM	Raiding party 2ND LT LAMB & 31 OR B Coy 2ND LT BEAUMONT [illegible] party [illegible] RE [illegible] Owing to Signal for artillery [illegible]	[illegible]
	19.3.18	3.15AM	Raid took place. Enemy [illegible] which put the BARRAGE [illegible] Reached [illegible] 2ND LT BEAUMONT [illegible] it was too light then for any [illegible] in A. A [illegible] place.	[illegible]
	20.3.18		Quiet day [illegible]	
	21.3.18	4.10am	Violent enemy bombardment. 5.25am [illegible] to "Take Action" [illegible] 6.40am to BROSSE WOOD to [illegible] positions. [illegible]	
	24.3.18		At PERONNE [illegible] fighting [illegible]	

2449 Wt. W14957/M90 750,000 1/16 J.B.C. & A. Forms/C.2118/12.

Army Form C. 2118.

Instructions regarding War Diaries and Intelligence Summaries are contained in F. S. Regs., Part II. and the Staff Manual respectively. Title pages will be prepared in manuscript.

WAR DIARY
or
~~INTELLIGENCE SUMMARY.~~
(Erase heading not required.)

Place	Date	Hour	Summary of Events and Information	Remarks and references to Appendices
MONTIGNY	20·3·18		Quiet day to-day	aah
	21·3·18	4·10am	Violent Enemy bombardment	aah
		5·25am	Verbal instructions to "take action" - Marched out at 6·10 a.m. to BROSSE WOOD to hold position. Entered combat line	aah
		6·30pm	Remainder of Battn consisting chiefly of "B" Coy fell back on Redoubts on flank of JEANCOURT VALLEY during night.	aah
JEANCOURT	22-3-18	6·15am	Violent Enemy bombardment.	aah
		9·30am	Enemy attacked on flanks. Withdrew to BROWN LINE. Remainder of Battn came under command of MAJ GRACEY R.E.	aah
		2·30pm	Enemy again attacked in large numbers. Attack held up for ½ an hour by M.G. and rifle fire.	aah
		3·0pm	199th BDE retired through MONTIGNY 2/7th MANCH. R. forming rearguard.	aah
		4·15pm	Fell back through dismounted cavalry and 50th DIV who were holding position E of BERNES	aah
		6·15pm	Arrive at BOUVINCOURT and join remnants of 199th BDE.	aah
		8·30pm	March out to DOINGT. On reaching this place MAJ J. ROWBOTHAM M.C. assumed command of Battn. Receive orders to proceed to BARLEUX	aah
BARLEUX	23·3·18	4·5am	Arrive at BARLEUX	aah
		9·0am	Battn reorganised.	aah
		11am	2nd LT A. WALKER & 2nd LT M.J.P. GAPP & 100 O.R. move up to PERONNE to hold bridges over R. SOMME.	aah

D. D. & L., London, E.C. (A7883) Wt. W803/M1672 350,000 4/17 Sch. 52a Forms/C/2118/14

Instructions regarding War Diaries and Intelligence Summaries are contained in F. S. Regs., Part II. and the Staff Manual respectively. Title pages will be prepared in manuscript.

WAR DIARY
or
~~INTELLIGENCE~~ SUMMARY.
(*Erase heading not required.*)

Army Form C. 2118.

Place	Date	Hour	Summary of Events and Information	Remarks and references to Appendices
BARLEUX	23.3.18 ~~20 pm~~	2.0pm	Battn. mans trenches E. of BARLEUX	a.a.h.
		4.0pm	Battn. moves up to BIACHES to reinforce 2ND LT WALKER'S party. Quiet night – Bombed by Aeroplanes.	a.a.h.
BIACHES	24-3-18	10.30pm	MAJ J. ROWBOTHAM M.C. Killed near PERONNE. Battn. comes under command of LT. COL. ~~[illegible]~~ MAXWELL a.a.h. 2/5th MANCH R.	a.a.h.
		1.30pm	Enemy observed this side of river massing for attack. Attack did not materialise. Quiet night	This attack was probably broken by our incessant M.G. fire.
BIACHES	25-3-18	10.0am	Enemy attacked our positions in front of BIACHES ROAD making use of Houses and shrubbery as cover. Enemy came into view when within 100 yards of our forward positions and met with severe rifle and M.G. fire and was repulsed.	a.a.h.
		12.30pm	Enemy again attacked gaining a footing in trenches on our left. Also penetrated line on our right.	a.a.h.
		1.30pm	Enemy observed in houses in right rear. Casualties have been very heavy to-day. Remnants of Battn fall back on trenches NE of BARLEUX Re-organise under MAJ WHITWORTH 2/6th MANCH R. and become absorbed into Composite Battn of 199th BDE. hereafter called 199th BDE.	a.a.h.
		6.0pm	Instructions received 66TH DIV will withdraw to HERBECOURT Covered by 50th DIV.	a.a.h.
HERBECOURT	26.3.18	8.0am	Enemy attacked 199th BDE fought rearguard action back to DOMPIERES.	a.a.h.
		12.0mdy	Enemy penetrated flanks BDE. Marched back to HARBONNIERES and dug in E. of village.	a.a.h.

Instructions regarding War Diaries and Intelligence Summaries are contained in F. S. Regs., Part II. and the Staff Manual respectively. Title pages will be prepared in manuscript.

WAR DIARY
or
~~INTELLIGENCE SUMMARY.~~
(*Erase heading not required.*)

Army Form C. 2118.

Place	Date	Hour	Summary of Events and Information	Remarks and references to Appendices
HARBONNIERES	27.3.18	1.0 p.m.	199th BDE under MAJ. GRACEY took part in counterattack on VAUVILLERS. BDE advanced in one wave, extended order. Met with heavy M.G. fire from left flank and left front. Advancing line was swung round changing direction half left. At same time enemy countered with an attack from original direct front. BDE was forced to withdraw to "jumping off" trenches. Quiet night	A.W.
"	28.3.18	4.30 a.m.	Orders received to evacuate HARBONNIERES.	a.a.h.
		5.0 a.m.	Evacuation carried out in orderly manner.	a.a.h.
		8.30 a.m.	BDE occupied railway W. of GUILLACOURT	a.a.h.
		3.0 p.m.	BDE retired to sunken road N.E. of IGNANCOURT. Quiet night	a.a.h.
IGNANCOURT	29.3.18	10.0 a.m.	Retirement to sunken road about 1 mile in rear. Quiet night	a.a.h.
	30.3.18		66th DIV. withdrawn from line and moved back to AMIENS area.	a.a.h.
			TOTAL CASUALTIES from 21.3.18 inclusive Killed 37 Wounded in action 214 Missing 321	a.a.h.
			OFFICERS' CASUALTIES:-	

KILLED
MAJ. J.E. ROWBOTHAM, M.C.
LT. P.H. LECOMBER
2ND LT. E. BLACKBURN

DIED OF WOUNDS
LT E. ENTWISTLE

WOUNDED
2ND LT. R.W. BEAZLEY
CAPT. N. EDGE
2ND LT. R. WILLIAMSON
" C.E. SCOTT
" M.P.J. CAPP
" J. BOWES
" A.H. GREEN
CAPT. J.N. HODGKINSON
2ND LT. A. WALKER
" A.S. HUNT

MISSING
LT COL W.A. BAILLIE HAMILTON
LT COL G. ROBERTS (LF ATTD)
LT A.G. ALDRED
" J.N. ROSTERN
2ND LT. E.H. SHAW
CAPT. & ADJ. J.A. SCHOFIELD
" T.W. LEIGHTON (RAMC ATTD)
" J. BROWN
2ND LT. R. STURGESS
" F.D. ANDREW
" C.H.D. RHEADE
" F.R. FREEMAN
" A. PRIME
LT. R.W. FOX
2ND LT. W. HASLAM
" J.M. HAYES, M.C.

SENT TO HOSPITAL
2ND LT. H. SHIRLEY
" H.R. MAWSON
" W. GALLPORT
LT. T.E. BRITTAIN

G. Hammond, Capt. & Adj. 2/7th Bn. Lancs. Fus.

D. D. & L., London, E.C. (A7883) Wt. W803/M1672 350,000 4/17 Sch. 52a Forms/C/2118/14

SECRET. [illegible] Bn. [illegible] Operation Order No. [illegible] Copy No. [illegible]

Ref. Map.
[illegible]

[illegible]

1. RELIEF. The Battalion will relieve the [illegible] in Support tomorrow, [illegible]. Companies will take over from opposite numbers.

2. GUIDES. Guides will meet companies as under:-

Unit.	Time.	Place.	Remarks.
H.Q. [illegible]	[illegible]	[illegible]	[illegible]
"[illegible]" Co.	"	"	[illegible]
[illegible]	"	"	[illegible]
[illegible]	"	"	[illegible]

[illegible]

3. [illegible] First Company will leave camp at [illegible]. Order of march [illegible]

4. [illegible] S.A.A. [illegible] Officers are advised [illegible] valises will not be taken.

5. TRANSPORT. The Transport Officer will arrange for limbers to report to Companies at [illegible]. Cooking utensils will be carried on these limbers. [illegible] and Canteen limber will report at [illegible]. [illegible] in Transport Lines.

6. WATER CARTS. Water carts will proceed, one with [illegible] Co., the other with [illegible] Co.

7. SURPLUS STORES. All surplus stores, officers' valises, [illegible] will be dumped outside the [illegible] by [illegible].

8. REAR PARTY. Lt. [illegible] is detailed as rear party. He will hand over camp to incoming unit and obtain receipts for all stores, defence schemes, etc., handed over.

9. SANITATION. The camp will be left scrupulously clean with fires burning in all [illegible], etc.

10. COMPLETION OF RELIEF. Completion of Relief will be reported to B.H.Q. by runner by code word "[illegible]"

11. Acknowledge.

(Sgd.) John A. [illegible]
Capt. & Adjt.
[illegible] Bn. [illegible]

Issued at [illegible]
Copy No. 1 Retained.
" " 2 [illegible] Brigade.
" " 3 2nd in Command.
" " 4 [illegible] Bn. [illegible]
" " 5 [illegible] Bn. [illegible]
" " 6 - 10 Companies.
" " 11 Quarter Master.
" " 12 Transport Officer.
" " 13 Medical Officer.
" " 14 R.S.M.
" " 15 - 17 War Diary.

SECRET COPY NO 15

2/7th Battalion Manchester Regiment

OPERATION ORDER NO 65 5/5/18

1. The Battalion will relieve the 2/6 BMR in the line tomorrow 6/5/18 after having been relieved by the 2/5th Bn. Manch R.

2. Companies will be relieved as follows:-

2/5 BMR	relieve	2/7 BMR
A	"	B
B	"	C
C	"	D
D	"	A
HQ		HQ

Guides will meet relieving Companies as under. One per Platoon and one for HQ Coy.

Guides from	Will meet	at	RENDEZVOUS
B 2/7 BMR	A 2/5 BMR	1·30 pm	L 10 a 0.8
C "	B "	1·45 pm	"
A "	D "	2·0 pm	"
HQ "	HQ "	2·5 pm	"
D "	C "	3·15 pm	L 26 d 05 05

3. Guides from 2/6 BMR will be at the EGG at the undermentioned times

A 2/7 who relieve	A 2/6	at 4 30 pm
B "	B "	" 5 30 pm
C "	C "	" 4·0 pm
D "	D "	under Company arrangements.

No movement from RED LINE till dusk

4 The following must be [illegible]

(a) [illegible]

(b) [illegible] and [illegible]

(c) [illegible] in progress and [illegible]

(d) [illegible]

(e) [illegible]

[illegible]

[illegible]

[illegible] be [illegible]

5. RATIONS

(a) [illegible]

[illegible]

[illegible] the VALLEY [illegible] 75

[illegible]

[illegible]

[illegible] VALLEY

[illegible]

[illegible] the [illegible]

(b) [illegible]

[illegible]

[illegible]

[illegible] TRANSPORT [illegible]

WATER

(a) [illegible] with

[illegible] the [illegible]

(b) [illegible] for Coy

and [illegible] (4) will also be

[illegible] and

[illegible] the following day.

(c) [illegible] Coys will [illegible]

[illegible]

8 [illegible] "NOTED"

9 ACKNOWLEDGE

[illegible] 10 [illegible]

[illegible]
Capt [illegible]

[illegible]

Copy	1	[illegible]
	2	1/9 [illegible]
	3	2/[illegible]
	4	2/[illegible] Bmk
	5	1/[illegible] Bmk
	6–10	[illegible]
	11	QM
	12	IO
	13	MO
	14	1 [illegible]
	15–17	War Diary

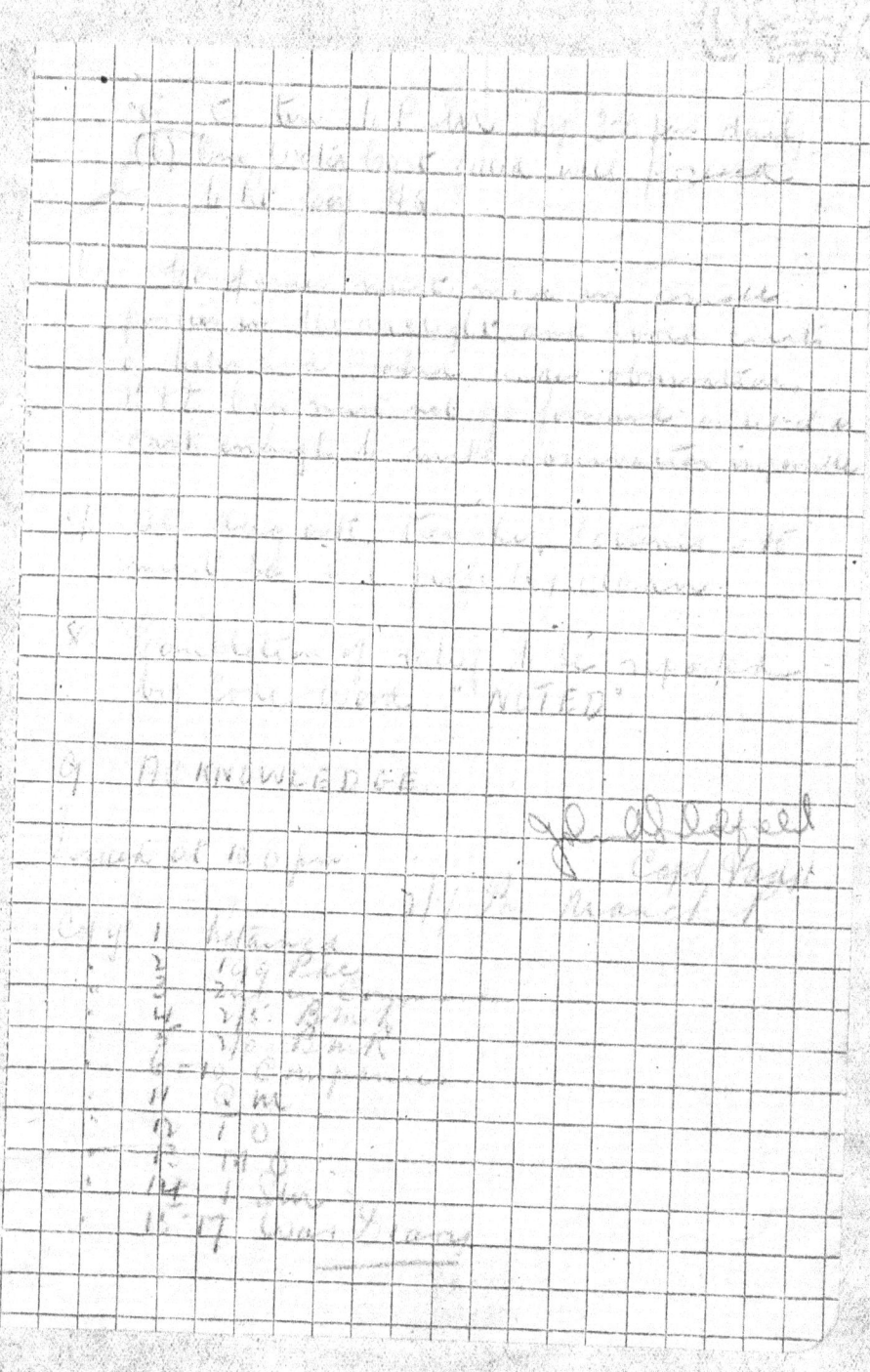

SECRET.

2/7th Bn. MANCHESTER REGT.
OPERATION ORDER No 66.

COPY No 14

REFERENCE 62c and HARGICOURT 1/40,000.

1. The Battn. will be relieved in the line tomorrow the 14th inst. by the 2/5 Bn. M.R.
2. Order of relief, guides and final destination of Coys. in accordance with Appendix "A" attached.
3. Transport for H.Q. A + B Coys (packs, stores and L.guns) will be at HARGICOURT DUMP as follows. 4 limbers at 4.30 p.m. 3 limbers at 6.30 p.m. 1 limber will report D.Coy H.Q at 7.0 p.m. C.Q.M.S. will arrange with R.S.M. for necessary trucks from line to DUMP. Trucks will be handed over to 2/5 M.R. at the DUMP before 9.0 p.m.
4. Lieut. Rostern will take over RESERVE camp at MONTIGNY and he will arrange for guides to meet H.Q. A. and B. Coys at night and guide to billets.
5. All trench stores, maps etc, will be handed over and receipts forwarded to B.O.R.
6. All particulars re Working parties will be taken over from 2/6 Bn. Manch. Regt. The Bn. will find no working parties on 14th.
7. All latrines, trenches and dug-outs will be left clean and fires will be left in all H.Qs.
8. Relief will be reported by B.A.B. code.
9. ACKNOWLEDGE.

John D. Schofield
Capt. & Adjt.
2/7 Bn. Manch. Regt.

Bn. H.Q.
13/3/18
ISSUED AT 6.45 pm

DISTRIBUTION.

COPY No.	1	Retained.
" "	2	199 Bde.
" "	3	C.O
" "	4	2nd in Command.
" "	5	T.O
" "	6.	Q.M.
" "	7.	R.S.M
" "	8.	2/6 M.R.
"	9-13	COYS.
" "	14-16.	WAR DIARY
" "	17	Lt. ROSTERN.
" "	18.	FILE.

APPENDIX A   REF HARGICOURT 1/40,000

COMPANY [illegible]	RELIEVED BY COY 2/5	GUIDES 1 PER PLATOON PLACE	1 PER HQ TIME	WHEN RELIEVED WILL PROCEED TO
A	A	THE EGG	6.0 PM	MONTIGNY
B	D	THE EGG	6.30 PM	MONTIGNY
C	B	THE EGG	7.0 PM	SUNKEN ROAD L 22 c
D	C	D COY HQ	7.0 PM	JEANCOURT (LESS 1 PLATOON AT BRUSSE RD HQ)
HQ	HQ	THE EGG	5.30 PM	MONTIGNY

Bn HQ
17/8/18

2/7th Battalion Manchester Regiment.

ORDERS for RAID NIGHT 17th/18th 191

Reference Sheet [illegible] 1/10,000.

1. **INTENTION.** To raid enemy front line trench between C 14 a 10.68 and C 14 a 80.40. To:
   (a) Account for as many Germans as possible.
   (b) Obtain indentifications (by prisoners if possible)
   (c) Wreck emplacements and dugouts.
   (d) Obtain positive or negative information about a suspected mine shaft.

2. **INFORMATION OF ENEMY.**
   (a) The enemy wire has been reconnoitred - a single belt - very dense.
   (b) There is a suspected listening post on the far side of enemy wire at C 13 b 90.70.
   (c) Machine Gun emplacement at C 14 a 08.68 and C 14 a 10.50.

3. **GENERAL IDEA.** R.E. party will leave our line at No.5 post C 13 b 88.90 before zero hour, and will place Bangalore Torpedo in enemy wire. On the explosion of the torpedo a silver rain rocket will be put up from MAIN POST. This will be the signal for a Box Barrage of 13 and 18 pounders to open. Howitzers and T.Ms. will fire at special targets. L.T.M.B. will open on left flank in continuation of Artillery Barrage firing on enemy communications.

4. **SPECIAL IDEA.** Raiding party will consist of R.E. party and 1 Officer 6 N.C.Os and 25 other ranks (split up into four parties)

   No.1 party of 1 N.C.O. and 4 other ranks will leave communication trench between No.5 post and German line, as soon as gap is made, rush through the gap and go down enemy line to the EAST, as far as junction Pt. C 14 a 10.68, and here they will make a block. No.1 party will take and lay a tape from point of exit from communication trench to the gap in the wire and on to enemy trench. This party will be the last to return and they will reel in tape, acting as a Rear Guard to the returning party.

   No.2 party, composed of 1 Officer 2 N.C.Os and 9 other ranks will go through the gap and work down enemy trench to the EAST till they come to first trench going SOUTH which they will go down as far as barrage permits. Dugouts will be bombed and M.G. emplacements destroyed. The emplacement at C 14 a 15.45 will be explored and accounted for before the party proceeds any further.

   No.3 party of 1 N.C.O. and 3 other ranks follow No.2 party down the trench going SOUTH until it comes to the first trench running EAST when it will make a block.

   No.4 party of 1 Sgt and 10 other ranks will follow route of No 2 party but will carry on to enemy front line working down as far as our barrage permits.

5. **WITHDRAWAL.** Officer i/c party will carry a whistle - long blasts at intervals will be the signal for return.

6. **ARTILLERY & T.Ms.** Heavy Artillery and T.Ms. will carry out harassing fire on their usual targets to hide the noise of getting the Bangalore Torpedo into position, from ½ hour before zero.

7. **ZERO.** ZERO will be the time of Silver Rain Rocket going up. The approximate time of ZERO will be notified later.

Issued at 7.30PM

[signature]
Capt & Adjt.

Copy No 1. C.O. Copy No.2 O.C. " " Co. 2/7th Bn. Manch. Regt.
" " 3 O.i/c. Raiding Party.
" " 4 199th Brigade. 5 - 10. 199th Bde. for distribution.
" " 11 - 13 War Diary.
" " 14 Retained.

Secret 2/7th Bn Manchester Regt Copy No. 10

Operation Order No 57

1. RELIEF The battalion will relieve the 2/8th Bn Manchester Regt in the left front line on night of 3rd/4th inst

2. DISPOSITIONS Dispositions in the line will be as follows:-

2/7th Bn	Location	2/8th Bn
A Coy	relieving right front line Coy	A Coy
B "	support "	B "
C "	left front line "	C "
D "	reserve "	D "

Companies will each leave behind an officer to hand over trench stores, details of working parties and work in progress to companies of 2/8th as follows:-

A Coy hand over to A Coy 2/8th C Coy hand over to D Coy 2/8th
B " " B D " " C

3. TIME The battalion will be clear of the line ZONNEBEKE X ROADS - ZONNEBEKE STA by 5 pm

4. TRENCH STORES All defence schemes, trench stores, details of work in progress etc, will be taken over and copies of receipts sent to Bn HQ by 12 noon on 4th inst

5. COOKS All company cooks at present in the line will report to the Master Cook at new Bn HQ at 4.0 pm

6. COOKING Instructions regarding cooking arrangements will be issued separately

7. R.E. MATERIAL Indents for RE material for work on front line posts must be at Bn HQ each evening by 7.0 pm.

continued.

8. SIGNALLERS. One signaller each from B & D Coys & HQ will report to Bn HQ at 1 pm. This party will proceed to new Bn HQ and will pick up one signaller each from A & C Coys. One signaller from each company of 2/5th Bn will report to company of 2/7th which they relieve at 2.0 pm to take over lines etc.

9. OBSERVERS. Company Commanders will each detail one observer to report to Intelligence Officer at new Bn HQ at 2.30 pm

10. SANITATION. All dug-outs, shelters etc will be handed over in a clean and sanitary condition both interior & exterior.

11. GUIDES. A & C Coys will arrange direct with 2/5th Bn about time & place for guides.

12 ACKNOWLEDGE

[illegible]
Lieut & A/Adjt
2/7th Bn Manchester Regt

DISTRIBUTION

1 199th Brigade
2 A Coy
3 B "
4 C
5 D "
6 R.S.M.
7 WAR DIARY.
8 "
9
10 FILE
11 [illegible]

4. Incoming Guides. Guides will meet outgoing Companies at BAVARIA HOUSE as follows:-
D Coy & H.Q. Coy 5 pm. A. B & C Coys 8 pm

5. Route. SEINE DUMP, CORDUROY TRACK, DEVILS CROSSING, ZONNEBEKE RD, FREZENBURG, DRAGOON CAMP.

6. Trench Stores. Defence schemes, trench & reserve ~~rations~~ stores will be handed over by Companies to relieving unit. All signalling equipment will be taken out, petrol tins which were brought up by Companies will be taken out by them.
Wet gum boots will be taken out, dry ones handed over to relieving unit.
Receipts to be forwarded to Bn. H.Q. immediately on arrival at DRAGOON CAMP.

7. Transport. Transport Officer will send two limbers one to be at SEINE DUMP at 5 pm. one at 7 pm to take Lewis guns, cooking utensils, petrol tins, wet gum boots &c.
First limber will be for all cooking utensils & stores of H.Q. & D Coy.
Second limber for stores of A B & C Coys.

8. March Discipline. A distance of at least 100 yds between platoons will be maintained.

9. Sanitation. Dug outs, pill boxes & surroundings will be left in a clean & sanitary condition.

10. Completion. Completion of relief to be notified by code words SEND PRISMATIC COMPASS.

11. ACKNOWLEDGE

[illegible]
Lieut. & A/Adjt.
2/4 R. [illegible]

8.2.18

SECRET. 2/7th Bn. Manchester Regt. Copy No. 10

Operation Orders No. 58

II

1. Relief. The battalion will be relieved on night of 9th/10th inst by the 5th Border Regt and will go by march route to DRAGOON CAMP moving to VANCOUVER CAMP morning of 10th.

2. Posts. All posts will be numbered according to new numbering & known & handed over by these numbers.

3. Guides. O.C. 'C' Company will arrange direct with O.C. neighbouring Coy. of 5th Borders all details of relief of posts 11, 12 & 13 on night of 9th/10th. A guide from each post 1-10 inclusive, 1A & 2A & Coy H.Q will be at HILLSIDE FARM at 6 pm on 9th to take in reliefs. O.C. 'B' Coy will detail an Officer to be in charge of these guides. He will report previously to Bn. H.Q for instructions.

On night of Feby 8th relieving Battn will send 1 Officer per Coy, 1 N.C.O & 1 guide per platoon to take details of line. These together with guides from this Battn will lead in relieving units to their positions.

Company Commanders should send guides to reconnoitre route to Zonnebeke Road before going out

SECRET. 2/7th Battalion Manchester Regiment. Copy a.

Operation Order No.59.

II

1. **MOVE.** The Battalion will move to Divisional Concentration Area to-morrow.

2. **STARTING POINT.** Subsidiary starting point will be road junction M.17.d.95.20., and Brigade starting point Cross Roads G.6.d.9.1.

3. **TIME AND ORDER OF MARCH.** The Battalion will parade in close column of Companies on open space behind Bn.H.Q. facing road in time to move off at 7-[illegible].am.
Order of march - "A", "B", "H.Q.", "C", "D".

4. **DRESS.** F.S.M.O. Instructions will be issued later.

5. **TRANSPORT.** Regimental Transport will march in rear of the column and will be at Vancouver Camp at 6-45.am.
Officers' Chargers will be at the same place at the same time.

6. **MARCH DISCIPLINE.** Strict march discipline will be observed, and distances as laid down in 4th Army G.S. 148 issued 8/1/18 will be maintained.

7. **INSPECTION.** The G.O.C. Division will see the Brigade march past on the road to the School Camp. Special attention should be paid to smartness of turn out and march discipline.

8. **M.T.** One lorry for conveyance of baggage will report at Brigade H.Q. at [illegible].am. on 11th inst.
R.S.M. will detail one guide to be at Staff Captain's Office at 7-15.am. to guide lorry to Bn.H.Q. where it will be loaded under arrangements by Q.M. This lorry will do two journeys if required.
Lt.J.H.Rostern is detailed i/c the first journey.

9. **BAGGAGE WAGONS.** Baggage wagons will report to Transport Lines on evening of 10th for the move and will return to their A.S.C. Company as soon as possible after arrival in the new Area.

10. **STORES.** Full establishment of S.A.A., Grenades, Tools etc. will be taken.
Officers' Valises and Company Stores will be dumped between Bn.H.Q. and road by [illegible].am.

11. **REAR PARTY.** 2/Lt.Andrew with 1 N.C.O. and 10 men of "A" Company will be left behind to clean up camp. This officer will obtain certificate from Area Commandant showing that the camp was left in a clean and sanitary condition.
Instructions to be obtained from Bn.H.Q.

2/7th Battalion Manchester Regiment
Operation Order No.5[illegible] (cont'd)

12. <u>SANITATION.</u> The camp will be left in a scrupulously clean condition and certificates forwarded to Bn.H.Q.

13. A C K N O W L E D G E.

Issued at ....

Lt. & Asst. Adjt.
2/7th Bn. Manch.R.

<u>DISTRIBUTION.</u>

Copy No.1 Retained.
" " 2 199th Brigade.
" " 3 O.C. "A" Coy.
" " 4 " " "B" "
" " 5 " " "C" "
" " 6 " " "D" "
" " 7 " " "H.Q.(a)" Coy.
" " 8 Quarter Master
" " 9 Transport Officer.
" " 10 R.S.M.
" " 11 Medical Officer.
" " 12 War Diary.
" " 13 " "
" " 14 " "

S E C R E T. 2/7th Battalion Manchester Regiment. Copy No. 12

Operation Orders No.80.

IV

1. **MOVE.** The Battalion will move from SCHOOL CAMP to HARBONNIERS Area on 18th instant.

2. **TIME.** The move will be by train. "A" "C" and "D" Coys. and Transport will move by train leaving PROVEN at 1-0.am. on 18th instant. "B" Coy. and cooker will move by train at 4-0.am. same date.
Transport will be at the station three hours prior to the hour of departure of train.
personnel one hour and a half hours before.
Companies will leave camp as follows :-
"A" Co. 9-30.pm. "C" Co. 9-35.pm. "H.Q.(a)" Co. 9-40 pm.
"D" Co. 9-45.pm.

3. **ENTRAINING.** Capt. Thody is detailed as entraining Officer and will report to representative of Brigade Staff at PROVEN Station a quarter of an hour before arrival of the Battalion.

4. **DRESS.** F.S.M.O. One blanket per man will be carried.

5. **STATES.** Complete marching out states will be submitted by T.O. Q.M. Os.C. "A" "B" "C" "D" and "H.Q.(a)" Coys. to Bn.H.Q. by 6-0.pm. on the 17th instant.
O.C. "B" Coy. will hand copy of his Marching out State to R.T.O. immediately on arrival at entraining station.

6. **DISCIPLINE.** Os.C. "A" and "D" Coys. will each provide picquet of one N.C.O. and ten men for front and rear of train respectively to prevent wandering at each authorised stop.
There will be a halt of about one hour at TINCQUES, about half way, for refreshments.

7. **LORRIES.** Two lorries will report at Brigade H.Q. SCHOOL CAMP at 4-0.pm. on 16th instant.
R.S.M. will detail a guide to report to Staff Captain before that time to guide lorries to Q.M.Stores.

8. **BAGGAGE.** Blankets, except one per man, will be dumped by 10-0.am. on the 17th instant at the Bn. Dump (Open Space N.W. of H.Q. Hut).
Stores and officers' valises will be dumped by 4-0.pm. on 17th instant.
L.G.Limbers will be loaded at Transport Lines before 4-0.pm.
Q.M. will arrange for all spare dixies to be transported to the station. Os.C. Coys. will arrange to draw these at the Station.

9. **MARCH DISCIPLINE.** Companies will march in file as far as road junction L.4.b.9.8., thence in fours to PROVEN, if the state of traffic permits.

10. A C K N O W L E D G E.

(Sgd.) J.A.Scholfield.
Capt. & Adjt.
2/7th Bn.Manch.R.

Issued at 4-35.pm.

DISTRIBUTION.

Copy No.1	Retained	Copy No.6	O.C. "D" Co.	Copy No.11	R.S.M.
" " 2	199 Bde.	" " 7	" "H.Q.(a) Co.	" " 12	War Diary.
" " 3	O.C. "A"	" " 8	Quarter Master	" " 13	" "
" " 4	" "B"	" " 9	Transport Officer	" " 14	" "
" " 5	" "C"	" " 10	Medical Officer		

17

[illegible]

[illegible] [illegible]

[illegible] [illegible]

[illegible] [illegible]

[illegible] [illegible]

5. TIME. [illegible]

[illegible] [illegible]

[illegible] [illegible]

[illegible] [illegible]

[illegible] [illegible]

[illegible]

[illegible]

[illegible] [illegible]

[illegible]

[illegible]

SECRET

Copy [illegible] 14

2/7th Bn. [illegible] R. ORDER. No. 62.

REF. MAP. SHEET 62c

1. MOVE. — The Battalion will move to HANCOURT to-morrow 25. 8. 18.

2. ORDER OF MARCH. — BAND & SIGNALLERS – "C" "D" "H.Q." "A" "B" TRANSPORT. Lewis Gun limbers will travel behind their Companies. One Gun will be kept prepared for action. The usual distance between Companies will be observed.

3. DRESS. — F.S.M.O. Soft Caps will be worn.

4. STARTING POINT. — The Battalion will form up in above order on the road on the EAST side of the Camp with the head of the column at the X roads ready to move off at [illegible] am. The leading Company will pass the X roads at VILLERS CARBONNEL ([illegible] 30 D 3.[illegible]) at [illegible] am.

5. ADVANCE PARTIES. — (1) Lieut. Rostron and 1 N.C.O. per Coy (5 Coys) will proceed to HANCOURT as Billeting Party. The N.C.Os will report to Lieut Rostron at [illegible] at Q.M. Stores. (2) Lieut. [illegible], the Transport Officer and 1 N.C.O. per Coy (A.B.C.D) will proceed to the FORWARD AREA by motor lorry leaving ABADIE CIRCUS ([illegible]) at [illegible] am 25.8.18. [illegible] N.C.Os will report to Lieut [illegible] at H.Q. MESS at [illegible] am. Rations for 25th and 26th will be carried. The party will visit the corresponding Battalion of the [illegible] Brigade in the line, and rejoin the Battalion on the 26th inst.

6. STORES — Blankets in bundles of 10, folded and clearly marked, tied up in [illegible], Officers' Valises and Company Stores will be [illegible] ready for loading at Q.M. STORES at [illegible].15 am. The Transport Officer will arrange for a limber to collect [illegible] and [illegible] at 8.15 am.

7. SANITATION. — The Camp will be left in a [illegible] sanitary and clean condition.

8. ACKNOWLEDGE.

ISSUED AT [illegible] pm

Copy No 1. Retained
" " 2. 199. Bde
" " 3. 2nd in Command
" " 4. O.C. "A" Co.
" " 5. " " B "
" " 6. " " C "
" " 7. " " D "
" " 8. " " HQ. "
" " 9. " " M.O.
" " 10. " " Q.M.
" " 11. " " R.S.M.
" " 12. " " T.O.
" " 13. War Diary
" " 14. " "
" " 15. " "

[illegible] Capt. & Adjt.
2/7th Bn. Manch. R.

Secret. Copy No

2/7th Battalion Manchester Regiment Order No.83.

Ref. Map Sheet
62c 1/40,000.

In the Field,
Feb. 28th 1918.

1. RELIEF. The Battalion will relieve the 8th Bn. Royal West Kent Regiment in Brigade Reserve at VENDELLES.

2. ORDER OF MARCH. Band, Signallers, H.Q. "B" "C" "A" "D".
Lewis Gun Limbers and pack mules will accompany their Companies, one gun will be kept ready for action.
Usual distances between Companies will be observed.

3. DRESS. F.M.O. Steel helmets will be worn.

4. STARTING POINT. The Battalion will form up in above order on the [illegible] ROAD with the head of the column at pt. Q 9 a 5.5. ready to move off at 8-0.am.

5. REAR PARTY. Each Company will leave behind a rear party to take officers' valises, blankets in bundles of 10, jerkins made up as last move, Mess and Company Stores, to Q.M. Stores after departure of Battalion.
O.C. "C" Co. will detail an officer i/c party. He will obtain a certificate from the Billet Warden that the Camp is left in a clean and sanitary condition before marching the party to rejoin the Battalion. He will report to the Adjutant at 7-30.am.

6. TRANSPORT & Q.M. STORES. Transport and Q.M. Stores will move independently to MONTIGNY and take over corresponding billets from 8th Battn. Royal West Kent Regt.
Orderly Room Limber will be at B.O.R. at 7-0.am.
Officers Chargers will be at H.Q. at 7-55.am.

7. RATIONS. Rations will be drawn by Transport from Brigade Refilling point on Light Railway at K 36 a 8.3.

8. GUARDS & DUTIES. "B" Co. will take over on arrival all Guards and duties. Details of these will be issued to Companies tonight.

9. TAKING OVER. Trench Stores, Defence Schemes, and Reserve Rations, will be taken over and receipts given. Copies of receipts will be forwarded to B.O.R. by 9-0.am. 28th instant.

10. COMPLETION OF RELIEF. Completion of relief will be reported to Bn.H.Q. by Runner.

11. A C K N O W L E D G E.

(Sgd) John A. Scholfield
Capt. & Adjt.
2/7th Battn. Manchester Regt.

Issued at 7-8.pm.

DISTRIBUTION.

Copy No 1 retained.
" " 2 199th Brigade.
" " 3 2nd in Command.
" " 4 O.C. "A" Co.
" " 5 " " "B" "
" " 6 " " "C" "
" " 7 " " "D" "
" " 8 " " H.Q. "
" " 9 Quarter-Master.
" " 10 Transport Officer.
" " 11 R.S.M.
" " 12 War Diary.
" " 13 " "
" " 14 " "

VIII

List of Officers transferred
from 2/8th Bn Manchester R.

Capt. Rhodes. C.J.
Lieut. Entwistle C.F.
2/Lt Mawson. H.R.
– Shaw. F.
– Bowes. J.
– Parsons. G.
– Walker. H.
– Harrop. W.J.
– Prime. A.
– Green. A.H.

199/66

WM 14

CONFIDENTIAL

WAR DIARY OF

2/7TH BN. MANCHESTER REGT.

FROM APRIL 1ST 1918 TO APRIL 30TH 1918

(VOLUME II)

Army Form C. 2118.

Instructions regarding War Diaries and Intelligence Summaries are contained in F. S. Regs., Part II. and the Staff Manual respectively. Title pages will be prepared in manuscript.

WAR DIARY
or
~~INTELLIGENCE SUMMARY.~~
(Erase heading not required.)

Place	Date	Hour	Summary of Events and Information	Remarks and references to Appendices
PISSY	1/4/18		Remainder of Battn join Transport Inspection by BRIG-GEN WILLIAMS	Aal
"	2.4.18		Battn entrains at SALEUX for LONG area. move into billets at AILLY-LE-HAUT-CLOCHET	Aal.
AILLY	4.4.18		Battn marches to COULENVILLERS	Aal
COULENVILLERS	6.4.18		CAPT. BOLTON on rejoining Battn assumes command	Aal
	10.4.18		Battn moves to CANDAS.	Aal
	12.4.18		Composite Company joins MANCHESTER COMPOSITE BATTN at COULENVILLERS	
			Remainder of Battn move to DRUCART Move Order No 3	Aal
	16.4.18		LT COL. DARBY GRIFFITHS M.C. assumes command of Battn	Aal
	17.4.18		Headquarters of Battn take over MANCHESTER COMPOSITE BATTN at LONG	Aal
	"		LT COL WARD McQUAID assumes command of Battn	Aal
	21.4.18		LT COL DE LA PERRELLE D.S.O. M.C. assumes command of Battn	Aal
	23.4.18		Battn moves to QUELMES Move Order No1.	
	25.4.18		Surplus personnel i.e. all ranks excluded from Battn training cadre, proceed to BASE under LT C.M. COOPER	Aal
	26.4.18		Battn training Cadre moves to LOTTINGHEM Cadre Order No.1	Aal
	28.4.18		Battn training Cadre moves to ESCOEUILLES Cadre Order No 2	Aal.

[signature] Lt Col.
Comdg. 2/1st Manchester Regt

D. D. & L., London, E.C.
(A7883) Wt. W803/M1672 350,000 4/17 Sch. 52a Forms/C/2118/14

SECRET.
No. of.
[illegible]

Manchester Composite Battalion
Move Order No.1.

Copy No. 15

1. MOVE. The Manchester Composite Battalion will move by train to [illegible] area in accordance with attached Time Table.

2. DRESS. F.S.M.O. Steel Helmets will be worn, Water bottles filled. 1 blanket per man will be carried in HORSE SHOE pattern over the top of the pack extending down the sides. Box Respirators will be carried on the top of the blanket on the pack.
March in column of threes.

3. ADVANCE PARTIES. 2/Lt. [illegible] will proceed by first train and report to the [illegible] at WIZERNES station for instructions re billeting.

4. LOADING PARTIES. (a) The following loading party will be detailed to report to R.T.O. [illegible] at time stated.
"B" Coy. 1 Officer and 50 O.R. report 15.00 on 22nd.
This party will travel by train No.14 on completion of loading.
(b) O.C. "D" Coy. will detail 1 Officer and 50 O.R. to travel by train No.9 and unload trains Nos. 9-14 at WIZERNES Station.
These parties should take rations for the 23rd.

5. MARCHING OUT STATE. O.C. "A" Coy. will hand to Brigade Entraining Officer on arrival at [illegible] a written Marching Out State for first train.
O.C. "C" Coy. will do the same for the second train.
Bn.H.Q. will do the same for the third train.
Marching Out States will be prepared at Bn.H.Q.
Figures should be handed in to O.R.S. by 9.0 a.m.

6. RATIONS. Rations for consumption on the 23rd will be issued to Coys. at 7.0 a.m. on the 22nd.

7. STORES. All Coy. Stores, Officers' Valises etc. will be carried on Coy. Limber, and Company Commanders are responsible that these Limbers reach entraining station at times stated.

8. BILLETS. All billets will be left in a scrupulously clean condition before marching out.

9. ACKNOWLEDGE.

In the Field.
22.4.18.

(Sgd.) A.Smithies.
Lt. & Adjt.
Manchester Battalion.

Issued at........

Distribution.
Copy No. 1 Retained.
" " 2 198th Bde.
" " 3 2nd in Command.
" " 4 O.C. "A" Coy.
" " 5 " "B" "
" " 6 " "C" "
" " 7 " "D" "
" " 8 Quartermaster.
" " 9 Medical Officer.
" " 10 Transport Officer.
" " 11 2/Lt. A.A.Lamb.
" " 12 R.S.M.
" " 13 War Diary.
" " 14 " "
" " 15 " "

Copy No 1)...

Secret.

2/7th Battalion Manchester Regiment.

Training Cadre Order No 1

In the Field,
26.4.18

1. **Move.** The Cadre and Transport of the Battalion will move today to [illegible].

2. **Starting Point.** Cross Roads ¼ mile S of E in [illegible].

3. **Time.** All personnel in present area will parade at Bn.H.Q. at 8-45.am.

4. **Dress.** Fighting Order (less Steel Helmets)

5. **Route.** [illegible] – BAYENGHEM – COULOMBY.

6. **Halt.** There will be a long halt for dinner at 11-50.am. March will be resumed at 1-0.pm.

7. **Stores.** Blankets will be rolled in bundles of 10, and loaded at Q.M.Stores by 8-0.am. also mens' packs. Officers valises will be at stores at same time. Transport will send one limber to H.Q.Mess at 8-15.am. for Mess baskets and C.O's valise, also half a limber to Bn.H.Q. for Office boxes.

8. **Billeting Party.** 2nd.Lieut.J.D.H.King and C.Q.M.S.Simons will be at BAYENGHEM CHURCH at 7-15.am. where a lorry will pick them up. This Officer will be responsible for billeting.

9. **Demonstration Platoon.** N.C.O's and men detailed for Demonstration platoon will report at Bn.H.Q. ready to move off at 6-30.am. Dress – F.S.M.O. blanket rolled over pack. They will report to C.O., 2/7th Bn.Manch.R. at [illegible] at 8-0.am.

10. **Sanitation.** All billets will be left in a scrupulously clean condition before marching out.

ACKNOWLEDGE.

(Sgd) A.Smithies,
Lieut & Adjutant.
2/7th Bn.Manchester Regiment.

Issued at 4-15.am.

Distribution.

Copy No 1 Commanding Officer.
" " 2 Quartermaster.
" " 3 Medical Officer.
" " 4 2nd.Lieut.J.D.H.King.
" " 5 2nd.Lieut.A.A.[illegible].
" " 6 Interpreter Roblot.
" " 7 C.Q.M.S.Simons.
" " 8 C.Q.M.S.Preston.
" " 9 Transport Sergeant.
" " 10 War Diary.
" " 11 " "
" " 12 " "
" " 13 Office.

Copy No [illegible]

2/7th Battalion Manchester Regiment.

Move Order No. [illegible]

1. Move. The Manchester Battalion (Composite) will concentrate at [illegible]villers today.

2. Starting Point. Where railway crosses road immediately [illegible] of [illegible] Station.

3. Route. [illegible]. 2/7th Manch.R. will lead and will pass starting point at 9.15.am.

4. Dress. [illegible]. [illegible] will be [illegible].

5. Command. On arrival at [illegible]villers, the Composite Companies will come under the orders of [illegible], 8th Manch.Rgt.

6. Rations. The Composite Company will take rations for [illegible] inclusive.

O.C. of this Company will notify [illegible] before [illegible] today the ration strength of Company.

7. Baggage Wagons. Baggage Wagons will report to Q.M.Stores by [illegible] today and will accompany Composite Company on march afterwards proceeding to [illegible].

8. Remainder. The remainder of Brigade will move to [illegible] (N. of Abbeville) passing same starting point as above at 9.15.am.

9. Billeting. 2/Lt. [illegible] will meet Staff Captain at [illegible] Church at 11.0.am to arrange billets.

10. Lorry. One motor lorry is allotted to the Brigade and will take stores for Composite Company afterwards will return for remainder of stores.

11. Sanitation. All billets will be left scrupulously clean and temporary latrines filled in.

12. Acknowledge. (Sgd) A. [illegible].

Lieut.& Adjutant.
2/7th Battn. Manchester Regt.

Issued at ....

Copy No 1 Retained.
" " 2 2nd in Command.
" " 3 "A" Co.
" " 4 "B" "
" " 5 "C" "
" " 6 "D" "
" " 7 [illegible]
" " 8 Transport Officer.
" " 9 Quartermaster.
" " 10 Medical Officer.
" " 11 2/Lt. [illegible]
" " 12 Capt. [illegible]
" " 13 [illegible]
" " 14 War Diary
" " 15 " "
" " 16 " "

Secret.

Copy No ...9....

2/7th Battalion Manchester Regiment.

Reference Map
Calais, 1/100,000.

In the Field.
27.4.18.

1. Move. The Battalion will move to-morrow by march route to ESCOEUILLES.

2. Dress. F.S.M. O.

3. Time. Parade will form up in time to move off from Bn.H.Q. at 8-30.am.

4. Stores. Blankets, Officers valises, etc, will be at Q.M.Stores by 8-30.am.

5. Transport. The Transport Officer will arrange for one limber to collect Officers' Mess kit and C.O's valise at 8-45.am also half a half to take Orderly Room boxes at same time.
The remainder of the Transport will report at the Q.M.Stores at 8-30.am to load up the remainder of the Battalion Baggage.

6. Sanitation. All billets will be left in a scrupulously clean condition before marching out.

7. Billeting. 2nd.Lieut. J.D.K.King will make all necessary arrangements re billets in the new area.

8. A C K N O W L E D G E.

(Sgd) A.Smithies,
Lieut & Adjutant.
2/7th Battn. Manchester Regiment.

Issued at 4-30.pm.

Distribution.

Copy No 1 Commanding Officer.
" " 2 Adjutant.
" " 3 Quartermaster.
" " 4 Transport Officer.
" " 5 Medical Officer.
" " 6 Captain M.Comey.
" " 7 Interpreter.
" " 8 2nd.Lieut.J.D.K.King.
" " 9 2nd.Lieut.A.A.Lamb.
" " 10 War Diary
" " 11 " "
" " 12 " "

CONFIDENTIAL

WAR DIARY

OF

2/7th MANCHESTER REGT.

FROM:- MAY 1st 1918 TO:- MAY 31st 1918

(VOLUME III)

Instructions regarding War Diaries and Intelligence Summaries are contained in F. S. Regs., Part II. and the Staff Manual respectively. Title pages will be prepared in manuscript.

WAR DIARY
or
~~INTELLIGENCE SUMMARY.~~
(*Erase heading not required.*)

Army Form C. 2118.

Vol 15

Place	Date	Hour	Summary of Events and Information	Remarks and references to Appendices
ESPUILLES	2.5.18		Battn. moves to Reserve Army at ST VALERY-SUR-SOMME Area. Cadre Order No 4	[illegible]
	3.5.18		Battn moves into billets at WATIEHURT	[illegible]
WATIEHURT	9.5.18		Battn moves into billets at LANCHERES	[illegible]
LANCHERES	11.5.18		Battn moves to BRUTELLES and affiliated with 3rd Bn 326 INF RGT US ARMY	[illegible]
BRUTELLES	12.5.18		LT COL DE LA PERRELLE DSO MC relinquishes command of Bn	[illegible]
	14.5.18		LT COL SIR GEORGE M. STIRLING Bt DSO assumes command of Bn	[illegible]
	22.5.18		Battn moves to MONTIERES	[illegible]
MONTIERES	24.5.18		Battn is affiliated with 2nd & 3rd Bns. 328 INF RGT US ARMY	[illegible]
	25.5.18		Battn moves to BOUBERT and is affiliated with REGTL HQRS & 1st Bn 326 INF RGT US ARMY Move Order No 50	[illegible]

Geo M. Stirling Lt Col
Comdg 2/7th Manch. Regt.

D. D. & L., London, E.C.
(A7883) Wt. W803/M1672 350,000 4/17 Sch. 52a Forms/C/2118/14

Secret. Copy No ....

2/7th Battalion Manchester Regiment.

Reference Maps. Cadre Order No.1. In the field,
Calais Sheet 13.) 1.5.18.
Abbeville " 14.) 1/100,000.

1. Move. The Battalion Cadre will move by rail to Reserve Army at St.Valery-sur-Somme Area, tomorrow, entraining at Desvres.

2. Time and starting Point. The Cadre will assemble with the head outside Bn.H.Q. in time to move off at 2-0.pm.

3. Transport. Transport of the Cadre, i.e. Water Cart, 1 Limbered G.S. Wagons and Main Wagon will proceed to Desvres in charge of 2nd.Lieut.A.A.Lamb and will arrive there not later than 3-0.pm.
The surplus transport will be disposed of in accordance with instructions issued to the Transport Sergeant.

4. Meals. The Cooker will accompany the Cadre on the march and on arrival at Desvres a hot meal will be provided before entraining.

5. Stores. Officers valises, Company boxes, etc, will be dumped at Q.M.Stores not later than 9-0.am.
The Transport Sergeant will arrange for half a limber to report at the Commanding Officer's billet at 10-0.am and for half a limber to be at Bn.H.Q. at the same time for office boxes.

6. Billeting Party. Lieut.L.J.C.Goodall R.Q.M.S.Hughes (D.C.M) C.S.Grant and C.Q.M.S.Simons are detailed as Billeting party. They will report at the Station, Desvres, at 11-0.am. and proceed by the first train leaving at 12-0.noon.
On arrival at Fressennville, (or detraining station) they will report to the Staff Captain for instructions regarding billets.

7. Sanitation. All billets will be left in a clean condition prior to departure.

8. Acknowledge.

(Sgd) A.Smithies,
Lieut & Adjutant.
2/7th Bn.Manchester Regiment.

Issued at 6-0.pm.

Copy No 1 Commanding Officer.
" " 2 Adjutant.
" " 3 Lt.L.J.C.Goodall.
" " 4 2nd.Lt.A.A.Lamb.
" " 5 Capt. McComey.
" " 6 Quartermaster.
" " 7 Transport Sergeant.
" " 8 War Diary
" " 9 " "
" " 10 " "
" " 11 Office.

Secret. **2/7th Battalion Manchester Regiment.** Copy No ..5.....

Move Order No. [illegible].

Reference Map Sheet
Abbeville. 1/100,000.

In the field,
31.5.18.

1. **Move.** The Battalion Cadre will move to-morrow from [illegible] to [illegible].

2. Time of **Start.** The parade will form up ready to move off from the Chateau, [illegible], at [illegible] a.m.
Dress- F.S.M.O. Waterbottles will be filled.

3. Stores and **Baggage.** Officers' Valises, Stores, Blankets, etc, will be dumped outside the Q.M. Stores by 5-30 a.m.
A Limber will call at H.Q. Mess at [illegible] a.m. and at [illegible] at [illegible] a.m. and will there wait for the column to pass.

4. Distribution of **Companies.** Nos. 1 and 4 Companies will be billeted at [illegible] and affiliated to the 3rd Battalion.
Nos. 2 and 3 Companies will remain at [illegible] and be affiliated with the 3rd Battalion.

5. March **Discipline.** The attention of all concerned is drawn to [illegible] M.39, already circulated, which must be strictly complied with.

6. **Sanitation.** All billets will be left in a clean condition, and the usual certificates obtained from billet holders that there are no outstanding claims for damages.

7. A c k n o w l e d g e.

Issued at 10.30 p.m.

(Sgd.) A. [illegible],
Captain & Adjutant,
2/7th Bn. Manchester Regiment.

Distribution.

Copy	No	1	C.O.
"	"	2	Adjutant.
"	"	3	O.C. No 1 Co.
"	"	4	" " " 2 "
"	"	5	" " " 3 "
"	"	6	" " " 4 "
"	"	7	R.Q.M.S.
"	"	8	R.S.M.
"	"	9	Capt. [illegible]. (C.F)
"	"	10 - 12.	War Diary.

Instructions regarding War Diaries and Intelligence Summaries are contained in F. S. Regs., Part II, and the Staff Manual respectively. Title pages will be prepared in manuscript.

WAR DIARY
or
~~INTELLIGENCE SUMMARY.~~
(Erase heading not required.)

Army Form C. 2118.

Place	Date	Hour	Summary of Events and Information	Remarks and references to Appendices
BOUBERT	1.6.18		Bn Cadre moves to WOIGNARUE to be affiliated with the 1st & 3rd Bns 326th American Inf. Regt. H.Q. & 2 Coy Cadres at WOIGNARUE; 2 Coy Cadres at ONIVAL with 3rd Bn. Training carried out with American Bns from 1st to 6th inst.	[illegible]
WOIGNARUE	7.6.18		Move order No 51 issued for move of Bn Cadre to ACHEUX to be affiliated with 327th American Inf Regt. Coy Cadres undertook training of affiliated American units as follows:– One with Regt H.Q. & H.Q. Coy at ACHEUX; one with 1st Bn at CHEPY; one with 2nd Bn at FRANLEU; one with 3rd Bn at MIANNAY until the move of 327th Regt (A.E.F) on 16.6.18 training was in progress with American Unit.	[illegible]
ACHEUX	17.6.18		Move order No 53 issued. Bn cadre moved to MONTIERES to be affiliated with 3rd Bn 105th Inf Regt (AEF). Training was carried out until 20th inst with this Unit.	[illegible]
MONTIERES	21.6.18		In accordance with Move Order No 55 Bn Cadre moved to QUESNOY ~~and~~ area (CAMPAGNE) with affiliated American Unit.	[illegible]
CAMPAGNE	22.6.18		Move to OUVILLE (HAUTVILLERS sub area) along with 3rd Bn 105th Inf Regt (AEF)	[illegible]
OUVILLE	23.6.18		The Cadre was detached from 3rd Bn 105th Regt and moved to EPAGNE to be affiliated with 123rd & 124th M.G. Bns (A.E.F)	[illegible]
EPAGNE	26.6.18		H.Q Cadre moved into AILLY LE HAUT CLOCHER to take over the administration of the LINE area Bgde group (Bgde Group Order No 1 issued). Coy Cadres at VAUCHELLES BUSSUS affiliated with 3rd Bn 129th Inf Regt (A.E.F)	[illegible]
AILLY	27.6.18		After moving to GORENFLOS Cadre was affiliated with units as follows. H.Q Cadre at GORENFLOS with Regt H.Q. & H.Q. Coy & M.G. Coy 129th Inf Regt. 4 Coy Cadres at ERGNIES with 1st Bn of this Regt.	[illegible]

[illegible signature]
Comdg. 2/4th Manchester Regiment

D. D. & L., London, E.C.
(A7883) Wt. W803/M1672 350,000 4/17 Sch. 52a Forms/C/2118/14

SECRET

Copy No 11......

2/7th Battalion Manchester Regiment.

Move Order No 51.

In the field.
6.6.18.

Reference Map Sheet
Abbeville. 1/100,000.

1. **Move.** The Battalion Cadre will move tomorrow, June 7th from Oignarus Area to the Acheux Area.

2. **Dispositions.** H.Q., Cadre, No.2 Company and all Specialist Instructors will be at Acheux.
   No.1 Company will be at Franleu.
   No.3 Company will be at Chepy.
   No.4 Company will be at Biannay.

3. **Dress.** Battle Order. Waterbottles will be filled.

4. **Time.** The whole personnel will parade on the main road, opposite the church, in time to move off at 5-45.am.

5. **Stores.** Officers' Valises, Mens' packs, blankets and Company Stores will be at Quartermaster's Stores ready to load up at 5-0.am. prompt.
   Two limbers from American H.Q. will report at the Q.M.Stores at 5-0.am.
   The drivers will be rationed for the day by this Battalion.
   One limber will report at Bn.H.Q. at 5-15.am and H.Q.Mess at 5-30.am.

6. **Sanitation.** All Billets will be left in a clean condition and the usual certificates obtained that there are no outstanding claims for damages.

7. A C K N O W L E D G E.

(Sgd) A.Smithies.
Captain & Adjutant,
2/7th Battalion Manchester Regiment.

Issued at 10-0.pm.

DISTRIBUTION.

Copy	No	1	Commanding Officer.
"	"	2	Adjutant.
"	"	3	O.C. No 1 Company.
"	"	4	" " " 2 "
"	"	5	" " " 3 "
"	"	6	" " " 4 "
"	"	7	[illegible]
"	"	8	Lieut.Goodall.
"	"	9	[illegible]
"	"	10	Capt.[illegible] (C.F.)
"	"	11	War Diary.
"	"	12	" "
"	"	13	" "

Secret.

Copy No ......

2/7th Battalion Manchester Regiment.

Move Order No.53.

In the field,
16.6.18

1. Move. The Battalion Cadre will move from the ACHEUX AREA to [illegible] to-morrow, June 17th 1918.

2. Time. Parade will form up in time to move off from the Church, ACHEUX at 8-0.am.
Detached Company Commanders will arrange to march independently.
Move to be complete by 10-0.am.

3. Dress. F.S.M.O. Waterbottles filled.

4. Stores & Baggage. All Officers' Valises and Blankets will be dumped at Q.M. Stores by 8-0.am. The Quarter-master will arrange to pick up Orderly Room boxes and Mess stores.
The limber will report at [illegible], [illegible] and [illegible] to pick up Officer's valises and stores.

5. Rear Party. Capt.Thody and the C.S.M. of No.4. Company will remain behind to hand over training facilities etc. to incoming Unit.

6. Billeting. Billeting Distribution lists and Billeting certificates already issued to Nos. 1, 3, and 4 Companies will be completed and stamped by the Mairie before proceeding to the new area.

7. Sanitation. All billets will be left in a clean condition and the usual certificate obtained that there are no outstanding claims for damages.

8. A c k n o w l e d g e.

(Sgd) A.Smithies.

Captain & Adjutant,
2/7th Battn.Manchester Regiment.

Issued at 11-0.pm.

Distribution -

Copy No	1	Commanding Officer.
"	"	2	Adjutant.
"	"	3	O.C. No 1 Company.
"	"	4	" " " 2 "
"	"	5	" " " 3 "
"	"	6	" " " 4 "
"	"	7	Quartermaster.
"	"	8	R.S.M.
"	"	9	War Diary.
"	"	10	" "
"	"	11	" "

Secret.

Copy No ....6..

2/7th Battalion Manchester Regiment.

Long Area Brigade Group.

Move Order No 1.

In the field,
26.6.18.

1. Moves will take place to-morrow in accordance with attached Move Table.

2. On completion of move the 18th Bn.K.L.R. will be under the administration of 198th Infantry Brigade Group, and the 7th Bn. Bedford Regt., under administration of 197th Infantry Brigade Group.

3. All moves will be by road unless otherwise stated.
No restrictions as to time and route.
Units will march early.

4. A c k n o w l e d g e.

Lieut-Colonel.
Comdng. LONG Area Brigade Group.
(2/7th Bn.Manchester Regiment)

Issued through
Signals at 7.pm.

Distribution.

Copy	No	1	66th Div.,H.Q.,
"	"	2	30th Div.,H.Q.,
"	"	3	18th Bn.K.L.R.
"	"	4	7th Bn.Bedford Regt.
"	"	5	Brigade Signals.
"	"	6	War Diary.
"	"	7	" "
"	"	8	" "
"	"	9	File.

Copy No ...8....

Secret.

2/7th Battalion Manchester Regiment.

Move Order No.35.

In the field,
21.6.18

1. Move. The Cadre will move from MONTIERES to QUESNOY le MONTANT today by march route.

2. Time. Parade will be formed up ready to leave the Chateau at MONTIERES at 7-0.am.
Dress. F.S.M.O. Waterbottles filled.

3. Stores, Baggage. All officers' Valises, Baggage, and stores will be loaded at Q.M's.Stores by 6-.15.am.
Limber will be used to carry the Orderly Room and Mess boxes, and will call round for these at 6-30.am. and 6-40.am. respectively.

4. Billets. All billets will be left in a very clean condition.

5. A c k n o w l e d g e.

(Sgd) A.Smithies,
Captain & Adjutant,
2/7th Battalion Manchester Regiment.

Issued at 1-30.am.

Distribution.

Copy	No	1	retained.
"	"	2	Commanding Officer.
"	"	3 - 5.	Company Commanders.
"	"	6	Quartermaster.

- CONFIDENTIAL -

VR 17

- WAR - DIARY -

OF

2/7th Bn Manchester Regt

From 1st July 1918 To July 31st 1918

VOL, XVI

Army Form C. 2118.

Instructions regarding War Diaries and Intelligence Summaries are contained in F. S. Regs., Part II. and the Staff Manual respectively. Title pages will be prepared in manuscript.

WAR DIARY
or
~~INTELLIGENCE SUMMARY~~.

(Erase heading not required.)

Place	Date	Hour	Summary of Events and Information	Remarks and references to Appendices
GORENFLOS	1/7/18	–	The battalion cadre was located at GORENFLOS, with 4 Company Cadres at ERGNIES. The HQ. of Cadre was affiliated with the Regtl HQ. of 129th American Inf Regt, & M.G. Coy and Coy. cadres affiliated with 1st Bn of 129th Amer. Inf. Regt. Remained with these units until their departure on 17th inst.	AS
FRANCIERES	20/7/18	·	The Cadre moved by march route to FRANCIERES	AS
HAUDRICOURT	22/7/18	·	Entraining at PONT REMY on 20/7/18, the cadre moved by march route & train to HAUDRICOURT, detraining at ABANCOURT. Awaiting instructions	AS
HAUDRICOURT	31/7/18		The battalion was disbanded as from this date. Authority G.H.Q. letter AG/4210/1 (O) dated 19.7.18	AS

G. W. Stirling Lt Col
Comdg 2/7th Bn Manchester Regt.

D. D. & L., London, E.C.
(A7883) Wt. W807/M1672 350,000 4/17 Sch. 52a Forms/C2118/14

www.ingramcontent.com/pod-product-compliance
Lightning Source LLC
Chambersburg PA
CBHW081404160426
43193CB00013B/2099